Identified, Tracked, and Profiled

Identified, Tracked, and Profiled

The Politics of Resisting Facial Recognition Technology

Peter Dauvergne

Professor of International Relations, Department of Political Science, University of British Columbia, Canada

 **Edward Elgar**
PUBLISHING

Cheltenham, UK • Northampton, MA, USA

Published by
Edward Elgar Publishing Limited
The Lypiatts
15 Lansdown Road
Cheltenham
Glos GL50 2JA
UK

Edward Elgar Publishing, Inc.
William Pratt House
9 Dewey Court
Northampton
Massachusetts 01060
USA

Paperback edition 2023

A catalogue record for this book
is available from the British Library

Library of Congress Control Number: 2022946665

This book is available electronically in the **Elgar**online
Political Science and Public Policy subject collection
http://dx.doi.org/10.4337/9781803925899

ISBN 978 1 80392 588 2 (cased)
ISBN 978 1 80392 589 9 (eBook)
ISBN 978 1 0353 2041 7 (paperback)

Printed and bound by CPI Group (UK) Ltd, Croydon, CR0 4YY

Contents

PART I   INTRODUCTION

1   Introducing facial recognition technology   2

2   Resisting the normalization of facial recognition   10

PART II   REINING IN FACIAL RECOGNITION
           TECHNOLOGY

3   The movement to oppose facial recognition   20

4   The politics of facial recognition bans in the United States   32

5   Regulating facial recognition in the United States   43

6   Rising global opposition to face surveillance   51

PART III   THE GLOBAL POLITICAL ECONOMY
           OF FACIAL RECOGNITION

7   The corporate politics of facial recognition   59

8   The everyday politics of facial recognition in China   69

9   The globalization of facial recognition technology   76

PART IV   CONCLUSIONS

10   The future of facial recognition technology   89

Appendix: interviews   97
Notes   99
Index   130

PART I

Introduction

1. Introducing facial recognition technology

Police in the city of Shenzhen, China, have long struggled to stop residents from jaywalking. To crack down, cameras with facial recognition capacity have been installed at busy intersections. The artificial intelligence (AI) powering this technology searches a government database to identify residents caught jaywalking, and then adds a dose of shame, projecting the name and face of the offender onto a large electronic screen beside the road. "Jaywalking has always been an issue in China and can hardly be resolved just by imposing fines or taking photos of the offenders," explains Wang Jun, a director at the AI company Intellifusion. "But a combination of technology and psychology ... can greatly reduce instances of jaywalking and will prevent repeat offences."[1]

No other country has gone quite as far as China in utilizing software to verify, identify, track, categorize, and analyze faces in videos or digital photos: a diverse array of technologies which, collectively, are commonly known as facial recognition technology (FRT). Cities all across China are using FRT to enforce traffic rules. Police in major cities such as Beijing are wearing facial recognition smartglasses and body cameras able to identify in real time anyone on a watch list. The city of Suzhou, 100 kilometers west of Shanghai, has even gone as far as deploying the technology to identify residents who venture outside in their pajamas – what city officials decry is "uncivilized behavior" – and then shame them on WeChat.[2]

More ominously, security agencies are using automated face identification to monitor residents in the region of Xinjiang in northwest China, the home of Muslim Uyghurs. Authorities are also using facial analysis software to "identify criminal suspects by analyzing their mental state," according to Li Xiaoyu, a police analyst from Xinjiang.[3] Elsewhere in China, authorities are using FRT to track anyone who looks Uyghur. The Chinese startup CloudWalk explains how the software works: "If originally one Uyghur lives in a neighborhood, and within 20 days six Uyghurs appear, it immediately sends alarms."[4]

School administrators in China, too, are installing FRT to take attendance and monitor hallways. One high school in Hangzhou has gone even further, using emotion recognition technology to scan facial expressions during lectures to check for signs of boredom, disbelief, sadness, anger, and skepticism. The system alerts the teacher when a "student is failing to focus during class time," said the school's vice-principal, Zhang Guanchao. It took less than a month for our "students to voluntarily change their behaviours and classroom habits," he added, allowing them "to attend classes more happily now."[5]

THE GROWING FACIAL RECOGNITION MARKET

China is at the forefront of facial recognition technology. All over the world, however, sales of this technology have been soaring since 2015. Detectives are uploading crime scene photos to identify suspects, witnesses, and victims with facial recognition software. Facial recognition drones are enforcing stay-at-home health orders to stop the spread of Covid-19. Schools are installing facial recognition cameras to alert staff if a known drug dealer, registered sex offender, or expelled student is lurking about. Facial recognition technology is automating border crossings and alerting authorities when undocumented migrants enter homeless shelters. Militaries are using the technology to detect unauthorized personnel and analyze drone footage. Security forces are mounting facial recognition cameras at political rallies, while retailers are deploying them to identify shoplifters and validate cashier-free purchases. People everywhere, meanwhile, are relying on facial verification and authentication to open apartment doors, access public toilets, and unlock iPhones and iPads. Even the security team for the singer Taylor Swift has used facial recognition technology to watch out for stalkers at her concerts.

Automated recognition of human faces, which has been under development since the 1960s, has become faster and more accurate since the early 2010s, as algorithms improve, computer power rises, and biometric databases expand. Quick and accurate computer verification, identification, detection, and analysis of faces, many people are now arguing, can do a great deal of good. It can add helpful features to consumer products, such as automatically grouping friends and family in a digital album. It can safeguard online transactions and prevent identify theft. And it can assist criminal investigators, as it did when identifying the shooter who in 2018 killed five people after storming the offices of the *Capital Gazette* newspaper in Annapolis, Maryland, and as it did when identifying rioters who attacked the US Capitol in 2021 during the Electoral College vote count certifying Joe Biden's presidential election victory.

Facial recognition technology, supporters are further arguing, can search crowds for a missing child or identify a lost Alzheimer's patient. Analysis of facial expressions with emotion recognition technology, some are claiming, has the potential to prevent suicides. And a live facial recognition system, many are contending, can sound an alarm if a known terrorist enters a shopping mall.

CRITICISM OF FACIAL RECOGNITION TECHNOLOGY

Many people disagree, however, seeing facial recognition technology as a grave threat to privacy, civil liberties, and human rights, especially for minorities and marginalized peoples. Some critics of FRT are not overly concerned about using the technology to access a smartphone or automatically organize digital photos in a personal album, as long as people can opt out and data protections are in place. Some also see value in allowing FRT to screen airline passengers or authenticate financial transactions through one-to-one photo matching, again as long as people can easily opt out, explicit affirmative consent is obtained, data protections are airtight, and information is not being collected for other uses. But, as interviews in 2021 and 2022 of policy analysts, lawyers, and activists with FRT expertise reveal, others worry the growing acceptance of facial verification (to confirm identities) and authentication (to confirm access or permission) is helping to normalize the identification, detection, and analysis of faces in publicly accessible spaces, which is reinforcing heavy-handed policing, invasive surveillance, and discriminatory corporate and governmental decision-making.[6]

In many ways, computer verification, authentication, identification, tracking, and analysis of faces are distinct technologies – relying on different algorithms and data and generating different benefits and risks for society – which explains why some experts refer to "facial recognition technologies" rather than "facial recognition technology."[7] Verification and authentication match a digital image of a person's live face (turned into a unique numerical representation, or faceprint) with a stored and labeled faceprint (i.e., one-to-one matching). Identification seeks to match a faceprint of an unknown person (e.g., from a live face, video frame, or digital photo) to a labeled faceprint in a biometric database (e.g., from a mugshot, driver's license, or watch list): what is often called one-to-many matching. Identification, which can occur in real time or after the fact, may produce multiple matches ranked by the system's confidence in the prediction.

Tracking follows a person as surveillance cameras capture their face-print, perhaps identifying them in real time by matching the faceprint to one in a biometric database, or perhaps by later linking them to a house address or license plate. Facial analysis collects information (e.g., frowns, smiles, glasses, and beards), infers emotions (e.g., anger, fear, sadness, worry, disgust, and surprise), profiles people (e.g., by race, gender, and sexual orientation), and predicts behavior (e.g., a person's potential for self-harm or violence) by analyzing faceprints extracted from videos and digital images (sometimes in real time and sometimes after the fact).

While recognizing these significant differences, policymakers and activists commonly refer to computer verification, authentication, iden-tification, tracking, and analysis of faces as "facial recognition." For example, the 2020 Act barring law enforcement agencies in Vermont from using facial recognition technology, except where the law already allows the use with drones, defines facial recognition as:

> the automated or semi-automated process that identifies or attempts to identify a person based on the characteristics of the person's face, including identification of known or unknown persons or groups; or the automated or semiautomated process by which the characteristics of a person's face are ana-lyzed to determine the person's sentiment, state of mind, or other propensities, including the person's level of dangerousness.[8]

Those campaigning to rein in FRT express a variety of concerns with the use of automated and semi-automated facial recognition for policing, surveillance, inferring emotions, predicting behavior, or determining race, gender, sexual orientation, religious beliefs, or political leanings. In their view, computer analysis of facial expressions and characteristics to evaluate emotions or predict behavior is an ill-conceived technology, no better than sorcery, while profiling customers or citizens with facial analysis software is innately flawed and prejudiced.

Using face identification and tracking for state surveillance of public spaces, they further argue, violates fundamental privacy and civil rights, as authorities remotely monitor residents without their consent or knowl-edge, in effect treating everyone as a suspect. Such surveillance, many are also arguing, does not respect core principles of necessity and propor-tionality in constitutional democracies, and risks creating a chilling effect on civil society. Those opposing the use of FRT for policing, school safety, and corporate security see many other dangers, too, including the potential for wrongful arrests, racist and prejudicial profiling, misuse of biometric data, and a deepening of systemic discrimination.[9]

As critics emphasize, facial recognition software in use in countries such as the United States commonly identifies white faces more accurately than non-white faces, and is especially prone to misidentifying black women.[10] "Even government scientists are now confirming that this surveillance technology is flawed and biased," notes Jay Stanley, a policy analyst with the American Civil Liberties Union (ACLU). "One false match can lead to missed flights, lengthy interrogations, watchlist placements, tense police encounters, false arrests, or worse."[11]

Computer scientist Joy Buolamwini, who in 2016 founded the US-based Algorithmic Justice League, has been at the forefront of exposing FRT's racial and gender biases. "We just assume because it's a machine or because we've used data that decisions are going to be somehow fair or neutral," she said. "But then we find when you look under the hood, something's rotten, and no one was checking in the first place."[12]

Even if facial recognition technology was to one day become "100% accurate," critics are further arguing, the potential for abuse would still be exceptionally high.[13] Imagine a political party monitoring every voter, all the time. Or a perpetual police lineup of hundreds of millions of people. Or an intelligence officer able for months on end to track a dissident as if they were in a hunter's scope: a scenario not far off in places such as China.

For Adam Schwartz, an attorney with the San Francisco-based Electronic Frontier Foundation, facial recognition technology is "a special menace to privacy, racial justice, free expression, and information security."[14] For Alvaro Bedoya, director of the Center on Privacy and Technology at Georgetown University, it "is the most pervasive and risky surveillance technology of the 21st century."[15] Woodrow Hartzog, a law and computer science professor at Northeastern University, and Evan Selinger, a philosophy professor at the Rochester Institute of Technology, go even further, arguing the "technology is the most uniquely dangerous surveillance mechanism ever invented."[16] Similarly, the ACLU describes it as "perhaps the most dangerous surveillance technology ever developed."[17]

OPPOSING FACIAL RECOGNITION

As criticism intensifies, calls for very strict legal controls on FRT are growing louder by the day. Privacy, civil rights, human rights, digital rights, and civil liberties organizations are at the forefront of the swelling resistance. This includes the ACLU (advocating for civil liberties in the United States), Fight for the Future (advocating for digital rights in the US), the Electronic Privacy Information Center (advocating for digital and human rights in the US), the Algorithmic Justice League (advocating for ethical, equitable, and unbiased AI), and the Public Voice coalition (which the Electronic Privacy Information Center set up in 1996 to support public participation in internet governance). It includes, too, OpenMedia (advocating for internet openness and digital rights in Canada), Liberty (advocating for civil liberties and human rights in the United Kingdom), and Big Brother Watch (advocating for privacy rights and civil liberties in the UK).

This is just a sampling of the organizations taking a leading role in opposing the use of facial recognition technology for identification, tracking, and discriminatory profiling. Elsewhere, the European Digital Rights network (advocating for digital rights in Europe) and the Internet Freedom Foundation (advocating for digital rights in India) are campaigning to rein in the technology. So are Access Now (advocating for digital civil rights globally), the Electronic Frontier Foundation (advocating for digital rights globally), Article 19 (advocating for human rights globally), Human Rights Watch (advocating for human rights globally), and Amnesty International (advocating for human rights globally).[18]

Many other advocacy organizations are participating too, from those fighting against discrimination such as Black Lives Matter to those advocating for gender equality and LGBTQ+ rights to those campaigning for labor protections and consumer rights, such as Brazil's Instituto Brasileiro de Defesa do Consumidor (Brazilian Institute for Consumer Protection). A diverse array of scholar-activists, social media influencers, artist-activists, youth organizations, and community groups are further energizing this collage of local, national, and international activism: what, in the most general terms, is a transnational social movement to oppose FRT, but which, in more fine-grained terms, comprises overlapping, interacting, yet frequently discrete, uncoordinated, local campaigns to demand stricter controls on the technology.[19]

Growing numbers of campaigns are amplifying the messaging and influence of the social movement to oppose facial recognition technology. Campaigns to rein in FRT go back many years. The 2009 Madrid Privacy Declaration, initiated by the Public Voice coalition and endorsed by 111 civil society organizations, called for a worldwide "moratorium on the development and implementation" of facial recognition technology for "mass surveillance."[20] Local campaigns have been proliferating since 2019, however, when San Francisco became the first jurisdiction to ban police and city officials from using FRT. In the United States, the ACLU and ACLU state affiliates have taken leading roles in local campaigns, supporting grassroots activism, drafting municipal ordinances, and providing legal support.[21] In other parts of the world, too, civil liberties, privacy, and human rights organizations have been organizing local campaigns to oppose the use of FRT by police, city officials, transit authorities, schools, stores, stadiums, and marketing firms, among others.

Numerous national, regional, and international coalitions and campaigns have also formed in recent years. In 2019, for instance, Fight for the Future, along with 41 participating organizations, launched the "Ban Facial Recognition" campaign to advocate for an "all-out ban" on the use of the technology by law enforcement in the United States.[22] That year, too, the Public Voice coalition drafted a declaration calling for a "moratorium on facial recognition technology for mass surveillance," which 112 organizations from around the world ended up endorsing, including Access Now, the Algorithmic Justice League, Article 19, Big Brother Watch, the Electronic Frontier Foundation, Fight for the Future, and the Brazilian Institute for Consumer Protection.[23]

In 2020, a coalition of 12 civil society organizations across the European Digital Rights network launched the "Reclaim Your Face" campaign to press the European Union (EU) to "ban biometric mass surveillance" (this coalition later grew to comprise 22 core members and 45 supporting groups).[24] The following year, Fight for the Future, along with 36 "partner organizations," launched a campaign to "Ban Facial Recognition in Stores."[25] That year, too, Amnesty International launched a campaign to "Ban the Scan," calling for a "global ban on facial recognition technology," and beginning with local campaigns in Hyderabad city in India (with support from the Internet Freedom Foundation and Article 19) and in New York City (with support from local organizations, including the ACLU of New York, the Electronic Frontier Foundation, and the Surveillance Oversight Technology Project).[26] Also in 2021, Access Now helped launch an international campaign to "Ban Biometric

Surveillance" and a campaign to "Ban Automated Recognition of Gender and Sexual Orientation" in the European Union.[27]

This is just a few examples of the growing number of campaigns to rein in FRT. Big Brother Watch, Liberty, Article 19, and Amnesty International are campaigning to ban face surveillance by police and private companies in the UK.[28] The Internet Freedom Foundation is calling for a ban on the use of FRT by police, intelligence agencies, and state officials in India.[29] OpenMedia is campaigning to ban the use of FRT by law enforcement in Canada.[30] In Europe, Reclaim Your Face campaigns are underway in the Czech Republic, France, Italy, Germany, Greece, the Netherlands, Serbia, and Slovenia.[31] Many other campaigns are gaining strength across Europe, too. Civil society organizations across developing countries in Africa, Asia, and Latin America are also calling for a ban on facial recognition surveillance, including in Argentina, Bangladesh, Bolivia, Botswana, Brazil, Burundi, Colombia, Costa Rica, Ecuador, India, Indonesia, Kenya, Mexico, Nepal, Nigeria, Pakistan, Panama, Peru, the Philippines, Myanmar, Thailand, Tunisia, and Venezuela.[32]

Indeed, campaigners all over the world are penning op-eds and initiating online petitions and open letters. They are investigating and exposing civil and human rights abuses. They are going to court to challenge the use of FRT by police, intelligence agencies, schools, and private companies. They are filing lawsuits on behalf of people wrongfully arrested following an inaccurate FRT identification. They are filing class-action lawsuits against technology companies collecting and storing faceprints without the consent, knowledge, or permission of users. And they are educating citizens around the world through social media (e.g., Twitter storms), online publications, and documentary films (e.g., *Coded Bias*, released in 2020).

What are the consequences of this social movement for the global uptake and uses of facial recognition technology? How are corporate and state supporters of FRT reacting to the growing calls for bans? Why is the global market continuing to grow for FRT products? What are the prospects of a worldwide ban on FRT for routine policing, mass surveillance, emotion analysis, and discriminatory profiling? The next chapter lays the foundations for fully answering these questions over the course of this book.

2. Resisting the normalization of facial recognition

The political power of the transnational social movement to rein in facial recognition technology is surging. The diversity of grassroots support and civil society organizations comprising this loosely organized movement is one of its greatest strengths. Drawing on a wide range of tactics, strategies, and support bases, the movement is generating political pressure across ideological divides, from multiple angles, and from a wide variety of societal sources.[1]

There are, of course, differences of opinion and emphasis within what can generally be thought of as the "anti-FRT movement." Importantly, however, as participation has been growing, the messaging has become stronger and more consistent.[2] Activists are continuing to expose the unreliability, inaccuracy, and algorithmic bias of facial recognition technology, especially when matching blurry video frames or forensic sketches with faceprints in incomplete or low-quality databases. Yet, with software engineers and facial recognition firms claiming these "problems" are "fixable," activists are increasingly emphasizing the innate dangers of FRT for civil society, no matter the degree of accuracy.[3]

Calls for permanent bans on the use of FRT in publicly accessible places, meanwhile, are growing louder as more activists come to believe that regulatory safeguards will never prevent abuses and as support for time-limited moratoriums wanes.[4] Many of those continuing to back moratoriums, meanwhile, appear to be doing so for political expediency – as a way of pausing the use of FRT until legal bans are put in place.[5] "We don't consider a moratorium to be a bad thing or a sellout, or a problematic tactic," explained Tracy Rosenberg, the executive director of Media Alliance. Instead, we see it as "a step on the way to a more comprehensive ban."[6] There is also an emerging consensus on the need to ban private businesses from deploying FRT in publicly accessible places, partly because of mounting evidence of privacy violations, data breaches, and rights abuses by stores and firms, and partly because of the risk of private companies selling biometric data and facial recognition services to state agencies.[7]

One example of this emerging consensus is the open letter released in June 2021 by Access Now, Amnesty International, Human Rights Watch, European Digital Rights, the Internet Freedom Foundation, and the Brazilian Institute for Consumer Protection, which calls for a permanent "outright ban" on governments and businesses using FRT in public spaces to identify, track, or profile individuals: what the coalition describes as "mass surveillance" and "discriminatory targeted surveillance" of minorities, dissidents, and marginalized groups. By the start of 2022, 193 advocacy organizations had signed the statement, including 83 from developing countries of Asia, Africa, and Latin America.[8] Support for the anti-FRT movement among citizens and politicians is rising, too, with governments and corporations around the world under increasing pressure from voters, consumers, shareholders, and courts to justify and restrict the use of facial recognition technology.

Broadly, I argue, the movement is diffusing a belief that FRT is highly problematic and should be strictly controlled. This belief, I further argue, is spreading and intensifying, and a global norm is emerging that governments should severely restrict, and in most instances permanently ban, the use of FRT for routine policing, mass surveillance, and discriminatory profiling in public spaces, including city streets, pedestrian pathways, parks, schools, airports, train stations, bus depots, stadiums, concert halls, retail stores, workplaces, libraries, public housing, and online platforms – what, in brief, can be thought of as the anti-FRT norm.

THE GROWING INFLUENCE OF THE ANTI-FRT NORM

Signs of the growing influence of the anti-FRT norm are everywhere. Since 2019 more than 20 municipalities across the United States – from San Francisco to Boston – have banned or strictly limited the use of FRT for policing and public services. The city of Portland, Oregon, has gone even further, also forbidding private businesses from deploying the technology in public spaces. At the state level, Maine and Vermont have imposed some of the strongest statewide restrictions, with Vermont, for instance, banning police from using the technology except with a warrant to identify a target in drone footage. States such as California, New Hampshire, New York, and Oregon have also banned some uses of the technology. The US states of Massachusetts, Utah, and Washington, meanwhile, have passed legislation to regulate the technology. Support for national regulation of FRT has also grown stronger among Democrats and Republicans in the US Congress, although progress toward legislation has stalled in recent years.[9]

Governments in Europe, too, are updating privacy laws and data-protection measures – such as the European Union's General Data Protection Regulation (in force since 2018) – and some governments are starting to put in place regulatory guardrails for deploying FRT for schooling, policing, and surveillance. In 2021, the European Parliament adopted a nonbinding resolution calling for a moratorium on the use of facial recognition technology for law enforcement (except to identify victims of a crime) until very strict protections, standards, and limits are in place; the resolution also recommended permanently banning the police from using private faceprint databases, such as ones built by scraping images from social media platforms.[10]

In 2021, too, the nonbinding three-party coalition agreement to form the new German government – between the Social Democrats, Greens, and Free Democrats, with Olaf Scholz as chancellor – expressed support for "ruling out" the use of biometric recognition for public surveillance (echoing the calls of scores of civil society organizations across Europe and at least 16 groups within Germany).[11] That year, the governments of Belgium and Slovakia also expressed support for a Europe-wide ban on law enforcement deploying remote face identification in public spaces, as did the European Data Protection Supervisor and the European Data Protection Board. "A general ban on the use of facial recognition in publicly accessible areas," the European Data Protection Supervisor and the chair of the European Data Protection Board said in a joint statement, "is the necessary starting point if we want to preserve our freedoms and create a human-centric legal framework for AI." The European Data Protection Supervisor and the European Data Protection Board additionally called for a ban on the use of FRT to categorize individuals based on gender, political orientation, ethnicity, and sexual orientation, arguing this is innately discriminatory and violates Article 21 of the EU Charter of Fundamental Rights.[12] The European Commission is also looking into ways to rein in facial recognition technology, in 2021 proposing an AI bill to limit governmental use. Internationally, meanwhile, in 2021 the United Nations High Commissioner for Human Rights urged governments around the world to "impose moratoriums on … remote real-time facial recognition."[13]

Corporations are conceding ground too, as when Amazon in 2020 suspended sales of facial recognition technology to police departments in the United States, and when Facebook in 2021 shelved its facial recognition tool for identifying people in uploaded photos (and deleted over one billion facial templates). Scores of music festivals and universities – ones such as Columbia, Harvard, MIT, Stanford, and Yale – have also now promised to never deploy the technology. The University of California Los Angeles (UCLA) has made this pledge too, abandoning plans in 2020 to install facial recognition security systems after a backlash from students and digital rights activists.[14]

Attorneys are also winning court cases and settlements against those deploying facial recognition technology. In 2020, for instance, in a case brought by Ed Bridges with the support of Liberty, the Court of Appeal of England and Wales ruled that South Wales Police was violating privacy, equality, and data-protection laws when deploying live facial recognition technology, which enables police to scan crowds to identify in real time individuals on watch lists.[15] That year, too, Facebook agreed to pay US$650 million to settle a class-action lawsuit claiming its facial recognition software for photo tagging violated the 2008 Biometric Information Privacy Act of the state of Illinois, which requires businesses to obtain opt-in consent before collecting biometric data.

THE UNEVEN INFLUENCE OF THE ANTI-FRT MOVEMENT

Zooming in, it may even seem as if growing resistance is going to contain facial recognition technology. Yet, as my analysis in this book reveals, the power of the anti-FRT movement is highly uneven, with disproportionate influence in North America and Europe, and relatively little influence in developing and emerging economies, including China, the world's leading producer, consumer, and exporter of facial recognition technology. Comprising a cacophony of voices with diverse concerns and cultural frames, the movement is noisier and more influential in liberal democratic jurisdictions with a robust civil society, strong civil rights and liberties, consistent rule of law, and a recent history of civil disobedience against discriminatory policing and mass surveillance. The movement's influence, moreover, is becoming increasingly uneven as the associational layers of resistance deepen more quickly in liberal democracies than in authoritarian regimes.

There is, to be clear, a loosely constituted global network of civil society organizations advocating for stricter worldwide controls on facial recognition technology, including across the developing world. But organizations and individuals from the West dominate. And, although resistance is intensifying in countries such as Brazil and India,[16] support for local campaigns in developing countries is comparatively weak, and at times even counterproductive, as authorities justify crackdowns by portraying local activists as pawns of foreign powers.[17]

To a small extent, ongoing differences of opinion among anti-FRT campaigners on the value and degree of regulation are further contributing to uneven influence, opening up opportunities for states and firms to undermine the messaging of more critically oriented organizations. Although the majority of anti-FRT campaigners are now supporting permanent bans, some activists and nongovernmental analysts still see strict regulatory measures as the best way forward, while a few are still calling for relatively light regulation, aligning more with the views of police, national security agencies, facial recognition startups, and corporations such as Microsoft and Amazon.

At the same time, powerful political and industry forces are pushing back against campaigns for bans and stringent regulation. Corporations are suppressing opposition, exploiting legal loopholes, and covertly deploying the technology. They are partnering with civil society organizations to call for industry-friendly regulation. And they are crafting a narrative that facial recognition technology is making life easier and safer for all.

Corporations and governments are also strategically expanding the technology globally. China is playing a leading role, offering loans and technical advice to help trading partners in developing countries purchase Chinese-made hardware and software for facial recognition systems. But the facial recognition industry across the rest of the world is also muting criticism by normalizing the use of facial verification, authorization, and identification in policing, schools, airports, and consumer products. Governments are further dulling criticism by framing facial recognition as a smart-city tool for protecting societies, while harmless for law-abiding citizens.

A few global technology firms such as IBM have shelved facial recognition products and services. Others, such as Microsoft and Amazon, are lobbying for industry-oriented regulation in markets at risk of bans or heavy restrictions, such as the United States and the European Union. Mostly, though, technology firms – whether from the US, EU, Japan,

Russia, China, or elsewhere – are working to thwart regulation. Adding to the challenge for regulators and activists, a growing number of facial recognition startups are navigating the global market as if there are no rules at all.

This book is the first to evaluate the global consequences of the anti-FRT movement. Activists around the world, as upcoming chapters confirm, are raising awareness of the flaws, biases, and dangers of facial recognition technology. Anti-FRT sentiments are intensifying and the anti-FRT norm is spreading. Activists are impeding the uptake of this technology, especially in political cultures that prioritize freedom and privacy, and with strong grassroots advocacy for democracy, civil rights, and civil liberties. And more and more governments are starting to put in place regulatory guardrails to protect privacy and impose limits on the use of the technology.

Yet, even as the power of the anti-FRT movement grows, for billions of people, especially those living in repressive regimes, the normalization of facial recognition technology for policing, surveillance, and profiling is picking up pace – a deeply worrying trend for the future of human rights, civil liberties, and democracy. My aim over the rest of this book is to explain why this is happening, evaluate the potential of anti-FRT activists to reverse this trend, and reflect on the consequences for global governance. A comprehensive review of the secondary literature on facial recognition technology and interviews with 30 policy analysts, researchers, lawyers, and activists in December 2021 and January 2022 inform my analysis.[18]

A GAP IN KNOWLEDGE

Many others have researched facial recognition technology. The 2011 book *Our Biometric Future*, by Kelly Gates of the University of California at San Diego, provides astute insights into why facial recognition technology was spreading well before it was even slightly reliable.[19] Stacks of books on the intensification of surveillance since the 2001 terrorist attacks on the United States touch as well upon the politics of facial recognition technology.[20]

There are also numerous journal articles investigating aspects of this topic. Searching the Social Sciences Citation Index of the Web of Science Core Collection, one of the world's largest journal databases, uncovers more than 200 articles published since 2016 on some aspect of the topic of facial recognition technology. Scholars are doing a particularly good job of probing the legal and ethical consequences of the technology.[21] Very few researchers, however, have investigated the growing societal resistance, and what this means for the spread of FRT globally. No other researcher, as far as I am aware, has conceptualized resistance to FRT as a transnational social movement. Delineating this movement in itself is an original contribution to the study of international relations, advancing in particular our knowledge of the consequences of civil society activism for the globalization and normalization of new technology.

Transnational social movements comprise nongovernmental organizations (NGOs), advocacy networks, and individual campaigners working both across and within societies to influence states, corporations, and social norms. Some transnational social movements are highly coordinated, with strong leadership, coherent international policy goals, and tightly linked members. Others, such as the anti-FRT movement, are loosely connected, decentralized coalitions of like-minded NGOs, grassroots activists, and individuals with similar goals, where influence on international discourses and local politics primarily arises from overlapping, reinforcing, yet largely parallel, uncoupled campaigns.

Contentious politics is at the core of transnational social movements: both the interplay of corporate, state, and societal politics and power dynamics among activists themselves. Historically, international NGOs have formed the core of transnational social movements: ones such as Amnesty International, Human Rights Watch, and Greenpeace. In recent years, however, local campaigners, grassroots protestors, and online activists have become increasingly influential, using the power of social media and online platforms to shame business leaders, pressure politicians, shift narratives, and inspire worldwide action.

At a very general level, the consequences of transnational social movements tend to be uneven, with activists having more influence in Western democracies than in authoritarian regimes, and more influence in wealthy economies than in poor, developing ones. Yet, as a deep dive into the politics of opposition to FRT reveals, preventing the normalization of a new technology is an especially difficult challenge for social movements, not only in despotic regimes and impoverished countries, but everywhere.

Transnational social movements have managed to push states to impose controls on some technologies, such as land mines, chemical and biological weapons, and blinding laser weapons in outer space, to name just a few examples. But activists have had far less success resisting commercial technologies where big profits are at stake. There are many reasons. Transnational corporations and startups tend to exaggerate the benefits and downplay the risks of new technologies. At the same time, technological diffusion tends to outpace the policymaking process, often dramatically so. Complicating matters, the social and environmental costs of the inputs for technologies such as computers (say, coltan or lithium) and outputs (say, electronic waste) tend to disproportionately harm marginalized communities and poor countries, distancing the consequences from those who are benefiting the most. On top of this, the full repercussions of commercial technologies may take generations to emerge, as with leaded gasoline and chlorofluorocarbons (CFCs).

The process of economic globalization, moreover, tends to accelerate the production and usage of commercial technologies, especially ones with diverse applications like facial recognition. Over time, increasing numbers of corporations start to market products employing the technology. And governments everywhere look for ways to boost manufacturing, sales, and investment. Consumers begin to rely on, expect, and eventually demand the technology. Engineers seek out even more applications, startups surface in every nook and cranny of the world economy, and the technology proliferates like a virus. Before long, the technology becomes normalized; living without it seems unimaginable, and shelving it becomes a stale, politically backward idea.

The difficulty of preventing the normalization of a commercial technology rises exponentially when, as in the case of automated facial recognition, the technology is a source of power. Almost always, ruling parties end up backing the technology. Militaries, police forces, and national security bureaucracies may end up doing so, too. Insurgents, criminal gangs, and individuals seeking power may even become major sources of demand, as we see with the normalization of handguns across much of the world.[22]

This does not mean that transnational social movements are never able to impede the normalization of a highly profitable commercial technology. The campaign to ban genetically modified crops in Europe shows this is possible even when powerful corporations and states are backing a technology.[23] Nor does it mean civil society uprisings cannot impede a technology that is enhancing the power of buyers, as the bans on semi-automatic weapons demonstrate in many countries. But, once a technology starts to become a normal part of life, the difficulty is far greater, as those who have been advocating for car-free cities know only too well.[24]

Many others have demonstrated the extraordinary difficulty of stopping the "creep" of technology toward normalization. Others, too, have noted the tendency of "technological mission creep" as organizations overstep authority, "function creep" as technologies take on new purposes, and "surveillance creep" as security agencies repurpose technology to ratchet up societal controls.[25] My analysis goes further, however, and looks more deeply into the unequal capacity of transnational social movements to stop the creep of new technology across different political, economic, and social settings.

In doing so, the book exposes the importance of political cultures, transnational corporations, power inequalities between activists and state–firm alliances, and cooperation within social movements themselves. To better understand these dynamics, Part II (Chapters 3–6) more thoroughly explores the politics underlying growing societal calls to rein in facial recognition technology. To begin, Chapter 3 outlines more fully the organizations, coalitions, and politics comprising the anti-FRT movement. Chapters 4 and 5 then delve into the politics of banning and regulating facial recognition technology in the United States, where civil society resistance has been particularly strong. Extending this analysis, Chapter 6 surveys the growing worldwide opposition to facial recognition technology, revealing the unequal global patterns of resistance, with civil society opposition strongest in Western democracies and weakest in repressive regimes (especially China and authoritarian countries in the developing world).

To better understand the varying consequences of the anti-FRT movement in different parts of the world, Part III (Chapters 7–9) explores the political and economic forces that are challenging critics, normalizing usage, and spurring global uptake. Chapter 7 investigates the corporate powers profiting from the technology. Chapter 8 examines usage within China, the world's largest national market for facial recognition products. And Chapter 9 documents the accelerating globalization of the technology. Chapter 10 concludes the book by reflecting on what the overall analysis suggests for the future of facial recognition technology.

The uptake of facial recognition technology, as Part III documents, is continuing to rise across much of the world. Yet uptake would be occurring even faster without the growing opposition to the technology. Activists have won many battles in recent years. The anti-FRT movement, moreover, is continuing to expand and the anti-FRT norm is continuing to spread. Certainly, the overall influence of this movement is highly uneven, but, as we'll see in Part II, this does not mean it is not making a big difference, nor that it will not make an even bigger difference in the future.

PART II

Reining in facial recognition technology

3. The movement to oppose facial recognition

In September 2020, city councilors in Portland, Oregon, unanimously passed an ordinance to ban the use of facial recognition technology by police and city officials, effective immediately. Then, again without any dissenting voices, and in a first for world politics, the Portland City Council passed a second ordinance, effective at the start of 2021, to ban businesses, such as hotels, stores, and restaurants, from deploying the technology in public spaces. "Technology exists to make our lives easier," said Portland mayor Ted Wheeler, "not for public and private entities to use as a weapon against the very citizens they serve and accommodate."[1]

Amazon had lobbied against the municipal laws. But this did little to sway city councilors, who concluded that automated facial recognition is biased, discriminatory, and a threat to the rights, liberties, and privacy of every resident of Portland. "All Portlanders are entitled to a city government that will not use technology with demonstrated racial and gender biases that endanger personal privacy," argued Mayor Wheeler during a city council meeting.[2]

Passage of the ordinances was a major victory for activists living in Portland. "With today's vote, the community made clear we hold the real power in this city," said Jann Carson of the ACLU of Oregon. "We will not let Portland turn into a surveillance state where police and corporations alike can track us wherever we go."[3]

Anti-FRT campaigners hailed Portland's ordinances as a big step toward eradicating facial recognition technology across the United States. "Now, cities across the country must look to Portland and pass bans of their own," said Lia Holland, a director at Fight for the Future. "We have the momentum, and we have the will to beat back this dangerous and discriminatory technology."[4]

Since Portland passed these ordinances, as we saw in the Introduction, jurisdictions all around the world have been enacting regulations, moratoriums, and bans to rein in facial recognition technology. Are activists on track to "beat back" this technology? Answering this question requires a fuller picture of the politics, organizations, and coalitions comprising the anti-FRT movement. Creating a picture of any transnational social movement is like trying to put together a jigsaw puzzle the size of a football field, when some pieces are missing, some are torn, and some don't fit at all. Worse still, the pieces are constantly changing shape, new pieces are always coming into play, and some pieces are fading away.

With that caveat, this chapter aims to piece together a picture of the anti-FRT movement, with the goal of then evaluating its influence in subsequent chapters. For background, I begin with a brief overview of the nature of transnational social movements within world politics.

TRANSNATIONAL SOCIAL MOVEMENTS

The past few decades have seen the associational layers of transnational social movements thickening as the number of NGOs grows and the internet amplifies voices of dissent from every corner of the world. These layers, as the Introduction mentioned, tend to be thicker in Western democracies than in authoritarian states and low-income countries. There are exceptions, however, such as grassroots activism for water rights, community advocacy for rights of nature, and direct-action resistance to corporate land grabbing, mining, and hydroelectric dams.[5] Pro-democracy movements, too, have swept away many ruthless dictators over the years. For most issues, though, the layer of civil society activity in repressive or impoverished regimes – not surprisingly – tends to be thinner.

Inside each layer, we find campaigners lobbying governments, shaming corporations, and organizing grassroots protests. We see them running research organizations, building websites, and launching lawsuits. We find them striving on social media to influence debates, sway public opinion, and propagate norms of right and wrong. And we see them building coalitions of like-minded groups to increase the size and scope of campaigns.

Some coalitions focus exclusively on local issues; others, commonly called transnational advocacy networks in the field of international relations, reach across national boundaries. Transnational advocacy networks are value-based, ideas-oriented associations of policy analysts, lawyers, scientists, writers, grassroots campaigners, and online influencers who are communicating and cooperating across sovereign borders. These networks support, interact, and overlap with local campaigns, with the lines increasingly blurred in the age of social media activism as the messaging of individual campaigners and international NGOs becomes progressively indistinguishable for the general public.

Nonprofit organizations employ some of the people participating in these networks. But far more of the participants are volunteers, contributing on and off while juggling the responsibilities of school or another job, including, possibly, working for a government or corporation. Advocacy on behalf of a government or corporation is not part of the internal politics of a transnational social movement, but rather part of state and corporate challenges to this politics. Business and state employees become part of a transnational social movement, however, when they step outside of their formal jobs to advocate for a political, social, or environmental cause – say, by marching in a rally, signing a petition, or hacking a website in the dead of night.

The politics of transnational social movements looks very different across issues. This politics also changes over time, as values and concerns shift, and as organizations come and go. Large, well-established international nonprofits – ones such as Amnesty International, Greenpeace, and Human Rights Watch – are at the core of some movements. Local resistance by marginalized communities energizes some movements, as with the right to water. Others are bottom-up, spontaneous uprisings, such as the Occupy Movement of 2011 and school strikes for climate action since 2018.

Coalitions of NGOs calling for worldwide action tend to have an easier time forming and growing when the campaign message is relatively simple – say, calling for a ban on chemical weapons or an end to commercial whaling – than when issues are complex and solutions are sharply contested, as with climate action or reproductive rights. Complex issues tend as well to draw more diverse perspectives into a campaign. Diversity of support can strengthen a movement by expanding its support base. But it can also create fissures, undermine consistent messaging, and splinter a campaign as adversaries work to divide and conquer subgroups.

Keeping these general features of transnational social movements in mind, let's now turn to delineate more precisely the organizations and differing arguments running through the anti-FRT movement.

THE POWER OF DIVERSITY

Since the early 2010s, the anti-FRT movement has been growing in size and reach, increasingly involving a more diverse array of civil society organizations from around the world. To amplify the voices of resistance, these organizations have been forming local, national, regional, and international coalitions. Volunteers and concerned citizens are a vital source of energy, and in some ways the anti-FRT movement is a bottom-up, grassroots uprising. Often, though, longstanding civil society organizations are supporting – and at times even coordinating – local campaigns. Many of these organizations campaigning locally and nationally, moreover, are also participating in transnational advocacy networks, which in turn are reinforcing the messaging and lobbying power of local campaigners.

As I mentioned in the Introduction, those advocating for civil rights, privacy rights, responsible digital technology, human rights, and civil liberties are at the forefront of the movement. At the same time, however, as public awareness rises, concerns deepen, and the use of FRT for policing, surveillance, and facial analysis spreads, the movement is broadening to also include, among others, those advocating for racial justice, LGBTQ+ rights, social justice, immigrant rights, faith-based ethics, consumer rights, and democratic freedoms.

This diversity is proving to be a great strength of the movement, generating a broad base of political support and empowering campaigns with the resources, experience, and people power of a large number of well-established civil society organizations. Significantly, cooperation has remained strong even as the movement's size and diversity has grown. At a basic level, everyone agrees that FRT risks harming civil society. Everyone agrees, too, that greater controls are necessary. What exact controls are best is still up for debate, although, as we'll see next, in recent years more and more civil society organizations have started to call for absolute, enduring bans on the use of facial recognition technology for routine policing, mass surveillance, and discriminatory profiling.

THE GROWING CALLS FOR BANS

Critics of facial recognition technology share several core general beliefs. They think the technology currently on the market is biased, discriminatory, and inaccurate. They believe the technology, no matter the degree of accuracy, has the potential to deepen invasive surveillance, cast a pall over civil society, and unfairly target minorities, such as Muslim Americans in the United States and Uyghur Muslims in China. And they see a need for much stronger laws to control the use of the technology for law enforcement, state surveillance, school and store security, business operations, predictive policing, emotion analysis, behavioral assessment, and the profiling of citizens and customers.[6]

There is less consensus, however, on how best to rein in facial recognition technology. Some are arguing for strict controls along the lines of managing hazardous waste. Some are calling for laws along the lines of wiretapping in the United States. Some are arguing for light state regulations along the lines of airline safety. And some are calling for governmental guidelines and corporate codes of conducts as the best way to maximize the benefits and minimize the risks of abuse.[7]

At the same time, though, increasing numbers of activists have come to the conclusion that comprehensive, permanent bans are necessary on the use of FRT for routine policing, mass surveillance, and discriminatory profiling, arguing that no regulatory system is ever going to prevent abuse by security forces, politicians, and corporations. Professors Woodrow Hartzog and Evan Selinger capture this sentiment well. Facial recognition technology, they argue, is "potently, uniquely dangerous – something so inherently toxic that it deserves to be completely rejected, banned, and stigmatized. ... The weak procedural path proposed by industry and government will only ensure facial recognition's ongoing creep into ever more aspects of everyday life."[8]

Facial recognition technology "is too dangerous to ever be regulated," argues Jennifer Jones at the ACLU of Northern California.[9] Trying to do so, Hartzog and Selinger add, will inevitably end up normalizing the technology within society, which would then smother any opposition. It must never "become too entrenched in our lives," they write. If this were to occur, "critics of facial recognition technology will be disempowered, silenced, or cease to exist."[10]

Luke Stark at the University of Western Ontario essentially concurs, describing facial recognition as the "plutonium of AI," and calling for "controls so strict" as to effectively ban the technology. "It's dangerous, racializing, and has few legitimate uses," he maintains. And in his view, this will never change, no matter how accurate it becomes.[11]

Growing numbers of civil society organizations agree, as interviews with anti-FRT campaigners in December 2021 and January 2022 confirm. Civil society organizations in Europe and North America are some of the most critical. "Face recognition surveillance presents an unprecedented threat to our privacy and civil liberties," the ACLU is arguing as it supports campaigns for local bans across the United States.[12] "Law enforcement use of face recognition technology poses a profound threat to personal privacy, political and religious expression, and the fundamental freedom to go about our lives without having our movements and associations covertly monitored and analyzed," the Electronic Frontier

Foundation is telling its base of supporters.[13] "We need to reinvest our resources and priorities into meeting the needs of our community, and not invest in dangerous surveillance tools like facial recognition," argues Myaisha Hayes at MediaJustice in Oakland, California.[14] The "technology is riddled with racial and gender bias," argues Ibrahim Hooper, the communications director for the Council on American–Islamic Relations, "and it should not be used by any government agency to target marginalized communities."[15]

Scores of other US-based NGOs are also chiming in to call for a ban on face surveillance technology. "The use of face surveillance technology needs to end. Face surveillance violates Americans' right to privacy, treats all individuals as suspicious, and threatens First Amendment-protected rights," argues Caitriona Fitzgerald of the Electronic Privacy Information Center in Washington, DC.[16] Not only do we need "a total ban on the use, development, production, and sale of facial recognition technology for mass surveillance purposes by the police and other government agencies in the United States," Amnesty International USA is telling its base, we need "a ban on exports of the technology systems to other countries."[17]

Civil liberties, social justice, and civil rights groups across Canada have taken a comparable stance. Coordinated by the International Civil Liberties Monitoring Group, in 2020 a coalition of more than 30 groups signed an open letter to the Canadian Minister of Public Safety and Emergency Preparedness calling on the federal government to ban the use of the technology by the Royal Canadian Mounted Police (RCMP) and national intelligence agencies. "Facial recognition technology is highly problematic, given its lack of accuracy and invasive nature, and poses a threat to the fundamental rights of people in Canada," the letter states.[18]

Liberty, the United Kingdom's oldest civil liberties and human rights organization (founded in 1934), takes a similar position. Facial recognition technology "breaches everyone's human rights, discriminates against people of colour and is unlawful. It's time to ban it," Liberty argues.[19]

Fight for the Future – an internet-based team advocating for responsible, open, and fair use of technology – agrees. "This inherently oppressive technology cannot be reformed or regulated," argues Evan Greer, the director of Fight for the Future. "It poses such a threat to the future of human society that any potential benefits are outweighed by the inevitable harms. It should be abolished."[20]

In 2019, Fight for the Future launched a campaign to "Ban Facial Recognition" in the United States. Today, the campaign comprises 41 groups, ranging from OpenMedia to the ACLU of New York to the Electronic Privacy Information Center to Greenpeace USA to the Council on American–Islamic Relations to the Black Alliance for Just Immigration. Those backing this campaign see the calls for state regulation and corporate self-governance as a ruse, designed to create false trust, deflect critics, and ultimately normalize a racist, biased technology for nefarious uses.

"Silicon Valley lobbyists are disingenuously calling for light 'regulation' of facial recognition so they can continue to profit by rapidly spreading this surveillance dragnet," the campaign to Ban Facial Recognition is telling the public. "They're trying to avoid the real debate: whether technology this dangerous should even exist. Industry-friendly and government-friendly oversight will not fix the dangers inherent in law enforcement's use of facial recognition: we need an all-out ban."[21]

A global coalition of digital rights and human rights similarly drafted an open statement in 2021 calling for a "global" ban on the use of remote biometric technologies in public spaces, including facial recognition technology. "We call for a ban because, even though a moratorium could put a temporary stop to the development and use of these technologies, and buy time to gather evidence and organize democratic discussion, it is already clear that these investigations and discussions will only further demonstrate that the use of these technologies in publicly accessible spaces is incompatible with our human rights and civil liberties and must be banned outright and for good."[22]

Access Now, a digital rights organization with teams across 13 countries and legal registrations in the United States, Belgium, Costa Rica, and Tunisia, has taken a leading role in coordinating this campaign. Five organizations joined Access Now in drafting the statement: Amnesty International, the European Digital Rights (EDRi) network, Human Rights Watch, India's Internet Freedom Foundation (IFF), and Instituto Brasileiro de Defesa do Consumidor (IDEC, or the Brazilian Institute for Consumer Protection). Within a month of its release, 174 civil society organizations from around the world had signed the statement. By 2022, the number of signatories had reached 193.[23]

CALLS FOR GUIDELINES AND GUARDRAILS

Others, though, do not think a permanent ban or heavy-handed controls, even for policing and intelligence work, are necessary or helpful. "Rather than setting down roadblocks to further innovation and use, we need guardrails to ensure the public and private sectors use the technology safely and responsibly," argues Daniel Castro, a vice-president at the Information Technology and Innovation Foundation, a nonprofit think tank specializing in technology policy.[24] What is necessary in the case of the European Union, Guillermo Beltrá at the Open Society European Policy Institute similarly argues, is the creation of "a sensible, legal, enforcement framework to govern" facial recognition technology.[25] Some want crime and anti-terrorism investigators to be able to use facial recognition software and surveillance when there is probable cause. Others are calling for a gamut of new regulations to ensure the technology is deployed responsibly.

Specific proposals on how to best govern FRT vary widely. Some of those calling for regulation want a specific ban on the use of the technology for general state surveillance of public spaces. Others are only pressing for a total ban on live facial recognition. Still others are additionally urging a ban on the use of facial analysis technology to infer emotions, predict behavior, and profile populations, arguing it is discriminatory and dangerously unreliable. Some distinguish between different uses of facial recognition technology, arguing identification for policing requires an especially stringent regulatory framework, while authentication for border crossings, online transactions, and retailing requires fewer legislative controls, as such uses pose fewer risks.[26]

Some proposals focus more on the need to protect personal privacy, advocating for stricter laws for collecting, deleting, retaining, and sharing information by government agencies and private businesses. Some focus on the importance of high security standards to prevent hacking. Some are proposing limits on the building and searching of faceprint databases. Some are calling for transparency, reliability audits, and accountability, including independent, third-party testing for bias. And some are demanding citizen rights to access and correct faceprint databases. A few proposals are going further still, calling on governments to make the sellers of facial recognition technology legally responsible for ensuring their customers use the technology appropriately.[27]

The alliances within and across transnational, national, and local coalitions vary widely, too. Those calling for bans tend to comprise like-minded organizations broadly advocating for civil liberties, human rights, privacy rights, and civil rights. Those calling for regulation sometimes include these same groups, but also may include industry associations, innovation and technology institutes, religious groups, and corporations. In 2020, for instance, the Vatican, with an endorsement from IBM and Microsoft, issued "a Rome Call for AI Ethics," which declares: "New forms of regulation must be encouraged to promote transparency and compliance with ethical principles, especially for advanced technologies that have a higher risk of impacting human rights, such as facial recognition."[28]

Microsoft is lobbying hard for industry-friendly regulations (and opposing outright bans) on FRT, and has aligned itself with a wide range of organizations advocating for regulated use.[29] "This is young technology," said Brad Smith, the president of Microsoft. "It will get better. But the only way to make it better is actually to continue developing it. And the only way to continue developing it actually is to have more people using it."[30]

This requires thoughtful regulation, not bans, Smith is arguing. Within the United States, he is calling on all levels of government to regulate the technology to protect privacy, avoid prejudicial uses, restrict face surveillance, and prevent a corporate race to the bottom. "We believe that the only way to protect against this race to the bottom is to build a floor of responsibility that supports healthy market competition," Smith wrote on the official Microsoft blog. Along the lines of how governments are regulating airlines and automakers, Smith has called on American lawmakers to regulate FRT following six core principles: "accountability," "notice and consent," "non-discrimination," "transparency," "fairness," and "lawful surveillance."[31]

COOPERATION AND STRONG MESSAGING

The efforts of companies such as Microsoft to lobby for industry-friendly regulation and seek out allies within government and civil society, however, are doing little to quiet the growing calls for comprehensive, permanent bans on using FRT for policing and surveillance. Nor are these efforts calming the growing backlash against the use of FRT for evaluating emotions, predicting behavior, and profiling sexual orientation, gender, and political orientation, among other traits.[32] Indeed, as interviews in 2021 and 2022 with anti-FRT campaigners brought to light, civil society support for time-limited moratoriums – to allow lawmakers to put in place regulatory guardrails – appears to be declining as growing numbers of activists conclude that guardrails will never suffice, as the risks of abuse are too high and the dangers of reinforcing over-policing, systemic racism, stereotyping, and unnecessary surveillance are too great. Importantly for understanding the growing power of the anti-FRT movement, this growing consensus on the necessity of outright bans for routine policing, mass surveillance, and discriminatory profiling is further helping promote cooperation, joint campaigning, and the consistency of public messaging.[33]

Differences of opinion and emphasis do continue to exist, as is always the case for any diverse and dynamic social movement. As mentioned, some activists are primarily concerned about the use of FRT for policing and mass surveillance, especially live street surveillance; others are just as concerned about the growing use by schools, stores, private businesses, and online platforms, including for both security and facial analysis. Some want blanket, permanent bans on all uses in publicly accessible places. Others see narrow bans on specific uses as the best – or at least the only realistic – way forward. There are varying views, too, on what, if any, exceptions to allow for law enforcement. Some, for instance, support limited, highly regulated use for investigating serious crimes, preventing terrorism, identifying victims of crime, searching for missing children, and identifying pedophiles from online images.[34]

To overcome differences of opinion, some anti-FRT coalitions are continuing to call for a "moratorium," without specifying whether the long-term goal is a permanent ban or regulated usage. This allows some groups to support the moratorium as a step toward implementing judicious safeguards, some to back it as a first step toward imposing very strict legal rules for policing, surveillance, and profiling, and some to support it as a step toward imposing a total or near-total ban on the development and use of all facial recognition technology.

Typical of the language used to build consensus, for instance, in 2019 more than 60 civil society groups – with ACLU leading the way – called upon the US federal government to impose a "moratorium on face recognition for law enforcement and immigration enforcement purposes until Congress fully debates what, if any, uses should be permitted."[35] That year, too, civil society organizations from around the world came together in Tirana, Albania, to pen a "declaration" calling for a worldwide "moratorium on the use of facial recognition technology that enables mass surveillance," and urging governments everywhere "to establish the legal rules, technical standards, and ethical guidelines necessary to safeguard fundamental rights and comply with legal obligations before further deployment of this technology occurs."[36] Revealingly, the Electronic Privacy Information Center and the Public Voice coalition, which organized the signing of the Albania Declaration, are also running a parallel campaign calling for a "moratorium" on the use of FRT for surveillance, which they call "Ban Face Surveillance."[37]

Ambiguity in the meaning of "moratorium" and "ban" – with the terms sometimes used interchangeably – has helped maintain high levels of cooperation among those campaigning to rein in facial recognition technology. Certainly, the behind-the-scenes politics can still be contentious within the movement – for instance, when those advocating for regulatory guardrails align themselves with firms lobbying for industry-friendly legislation. Overall, though, the movement is highly cooperative, with a growing and increasingly diverse base of well-established civil society organizations, and a solidifying consensus on the necessity of comprehensive, permanent bans on the use of FRT for routine policing, mass surveillance, and discriminatory profiling. Its global reach, however, remains highly uneven, with the unevenness increasing in recent years.

UNEVEN GLOBAL RESISTANCE

The anti-FRT movement is strongest in democracies that prioritize individual liberty and freedoms. Local resistance has been particularly intense in the United States, where the motto of New Hampshire is "live free or die," the motto of Delaware is "liberty and independence," and the motto of Iowa is "our liberties we prize and our rights we will maintain." The movement is weaker in democratic political cultures, such as in East and Southeast Asia, where more weight is given to community rights, social stability, and filial piety. And the movement is hardly visible at all in highly repressive regimes. Looking geographically, the associational layer resisting facial recognition technology is thickest over North America and Europe, and relatively thin over Asia, Africa, and Latin America.[38]

We can see this when looking at the 2019 Albania Declaration calling for a worldwide moratorium on face surveillance. Of the 112 signatories, nearly one-third are headquartered in the United States, while 10 percent are based in the United Kingdom. Relatively few organizations, meanwhile, are from the developing world. No organization signed from

China. Fourteen organizations did sign from Latin America; but, only eight signed from the Asia-Pacific region (Fiji, Kazakhstan, South Korea, Taiwan, two from Pakistan, and two from Australia) and just three from Africa (Côte d'Ivoire, Uganda, and South Africa).[39]

Since 2019, resistance has been growing in some developing countries, such as India.[40] And the overall reach of the anti-FRT movement into the developing world does appear to be slowly increasing.[41] Indicative, more than 40 percent of civil society organizations signing a 2021 open letter calling for a worldwide ban on biometric surveillance were located in developing countries in Asia, Africa, and Latin America.[42]

Still, the vast majority of developing-country organizations signing such open letters are merely expressing support, and organizations headquartered in Europe and North America are far more active and influential within the overall anti-FRT movement. Adding further to the movement's uneven influence, those organizations working to diffuse the anti-FRT norm are navigating markedly different local and national political settings. There are large numbers of local groups advocating for civil rights and civil liberties in cities such as San Francisco, and these groups can form powerful lobbying and voting blocs. In jurisdictions such as the European Union, too, there are large numbers of well-established civil society organizations advocating for human rights, privacy, digital rights, civil liberties, and civil rights.

Across the emerging and developing economies of Asia, Africa, and Latin America, meanwhile, relatively few local groups are actively and regularly participating in the transnational social movement opposing facial recognition technology. Many regions do not have civil rights, human rights, or civil liberties organizations strong enough to wage local action. And, in many places with a capacity to do so, states are suppressing voices of dissent.

This great variety of civic politics, along with the far deeper associational layers of anti-FRT resistance across Europe and North America, helps explain why, as we'll see over the rest of this book, there is very strong opposition and legal bans in some places and little to no opposition or regulatory controls in most of the world. The strongest resistance, as the next chapter discusses, has been in the United States.

4. The politics of facial recognition bans in the United States

Lockport City School District in upper state New York activated its facial and gun recognition security system at the beginning of 2020. This is going to prevent "school shootings," superintendent Michelle Bradley assured parents and students across her district's eight elementary, junior, and senior schools. One student at Lockport High School, asked what she thought of the new cameras, was nonchalant: "I'm not sure where they are in the school or even think I've seen them." Another student, asked the same question, thought the technology was "cool."[1]

Some parents and students did try to stop the district from deploying the technology. One father, Jim Shultz, called it a "colossal waste of money" and "an unprecedented invasion of privacy."[2] Civil liberties activists were equally critical. "Subjecting 5-year-olds to this technology will not make anyone safer," argued Stefanie Coyle of the New York Civil Liberties Union, "and we can't allow invasive surveillance to become the norm in our public spaces."[3]

Opponents did not give up, however, after the Lockport City School District turned on its facial security system. Since 2018, they had been penning op-eds on the inaccuracy and bias of facial recognition software, the risks to privacy, and the danger of exacerbating racial inequities in school discipline. They had been petitioning school administrators and networking with teachers' unions. And they had been lobbying legislators and finding allies within the New York State Assembly and Senate.

Resistance grew stronger even in the midst of the Covid-19 pandemic. Parents opposing the facial security system ran for Lockport school board seats, with Renee Cheatham, an outspoken critic, winning in June 2020.[4] That month the campaign intensified further when the New York Civil Liberties Union, on behalf of Jim Shultz and Renee Cheatham, filed a lawsuit against the New York State Education Department for authorizing Lockport's facial security system.

A month later, with the voices of opposition louder than ever, the New York State Legislature passed legislation imposing a two-year moratorium on purchasing or using facial recognition technology in New York State schools. The legislation, which then New York governor Andrew Cuomo signed into law in December 2020, requires the New York State Education Department to evaluate the technology, consult the public, and, if deemed appropriate for school use, propose a regulatory framework. It also forced the Lockport City School District to deactivate its facial recognition software. "We've said for years that facial recognition and other biometric surveillance technologies have no place in schools," said Coyle, "and this is a monumental leap forward to protect students from this kind of invasive surveillance."[5]

This victory in New York State, as this chapter shows, is just one of many for US activists in recent years. To better understand where and why the anti-FRT norm is intensifying in the United States, let's begin in San Francisco, the world's first jurisdiction to forbid its police and municipal agencies from using facial recognition technology.

THE ORDINANCE TO STOP SECRET SURVEILLANCE

By an 8 to 1 vote, the San Francisco city council – known as the Board of Supervisors – passed a motion in May 2019 popularly called "Stop Secret Surveillance." Broadly, the ordinance, titled the "Administrative Code on the Acquisition of Surveillance Technology," constrains the city's capacity to deploy all surveillance technology. "Legally enforceable safeguards, including robust transparency, oversight, and accountability measures, must be in place to protect civil rights and civil liberties before any surveillance technology is deployed," the ordinance declares. Specifically, it makes it "unlawful" for any city official or department "to obtain, retain, access, or use" facial recognition technology (or use any information from this technology).[6]

Advocates of this ban came from all walks of life. Unlike some American cities and federal agencies, San Francisco had not used facial recognition software to identity suspects from surveillance footage or police bodycams. But the San Francisco police department had used it between 2013 and 2017 to search its database of mugshots.[7] And San Francisco's history of covert surveillance of the civil rights movement had left many long-time residents nervous. Community activists felt it was only a matter of time before the city would start deploying facial recognition for mass surveillance.[8]

Some feared such surveillance would have a chilling effect on San Francisco's culture of civil society association and expressive individualism. Some saw the technology as a threat to privacy and individual rights, especially its ability to track law-abiding citizens without affirmative (explicit and voluntary) consent. Some were concerned with the potential of the technology to misidentify faces in video footage and contribute to wrongful arrests. Others worried the technology, regardless of its accuracy, would reinforce racist and discriminatory policing. Still others were afraid authorities would deploy the technology to search databases of driver's licenses, passports, online videos, and social media photos to harass minorities or deport undocumented migrants.[9]

The ACLU played a leading role in forming a coalition of 26 activist organizations calling for the ban. The coalition included advocates of civil rights and liberties, privacy and digital rights, LGBTQ+ rights, racial and social justice, and immigrant rights. The ordinance was drafted by Brian Hofer, a privacy advocate who is the executive director of the nonprofit Secure Justice, and Matt Cagle, an attorney with the ACLU of Northern California. They modeled the ordinance after an ACLU template to support city motions to ban facial recognition technology.[10]

After the ordinance passed, the coalition of 26 activist organizations put out a statement: "We applaud the San Francisco Board of Supervisors for bringing democratic oversight to surveillance technology, and for recognizing that face surveillance is incompatible with a healthy democracy."[11] Matt Cagle and the ACLU also saw this ordinance as paving the way for similar measures across the country. "The desire not to be tracked when you walk down the street or watch-listed by a secret algorithm, these are shared values across the United States," Cagle said. "We fully expect this vote and this ordinance to inspire other communities to take control of these important decisions."[12]

Campaigners in San Francisco were able to build a broad political consensus on the value of this ban. Critically, they convinced Aaron Peskin, the dean of the San Francisco Board of Supervisors, to sponsor the bill. For Peskin, San Francisco has a special responsibility to set high regulatory standards for new technology. "I think part of San Francisco being the real and perceived headquarters for all things tech also comes with a responsibility for its local legislators," he said. "We have an outsize responsibility to regulate the excesses of technology precisely because they are headquartered here."[13]

PUSHBACK IN SAN FRANCISCO

Not everyone in San Francisco is applauding the ban as an example of responsible governance. Some think it's heavy-handed, unlikely to remain in place in the long run, and unnecessarily forbids the many ways the technology could improve policing and city services. "It is ridiculous to deny the value of this technology in securing airports and border installations," said Jonathan Turley, a law professor at George Washington University. "It is hard to deny that there is a public safety value to this technology."[14]

Similarly, Daniel Castro, a vice-president at the Information and Technology Innovation Foundation, believes that San Francisco's ordinance is misguided. "The right approach is to implement safeguards on the use of technology rather than prohibitions," he said in statement opposing the ordinance. "Good oversight and proper guidance can ensure that police and other government agencies use facial recognition appropriately."[15] In his view, moreover, those claiming facial recognition technology is racist are relying on "shoddy" research and overlooking the exceptional accuracy of the latest systems. Why, he muses in an article titled "The Case for Facial Recognition," would a rational society not want a highly reliable technology to solve murders, find missing children, prevent school shootings, and protect government facilities from terrorists? "Instead of supporting the calls for bans," he argues, "policymakers should create rules to prevent inappropriate uses of facial recognition technology by government and allow government to adopt the technology where it is useful."[16]

The San Francisco Police Officers Association also opposed the ban, arguing facial recognition technology can provide invaluable leads for investigators, and is only going to become more accurate with each passing year. Tech industry lobbyists made a case as well for the value of the technology, although firms such as Microsoft, Amazon, and NEC kept a low profile to avoid attracting the ire of activists and maintain their focus on pressing for industry-friendly regulations in jurisdictions with less civil society opposition to the technology.[17] The biometrics industry lobbied against the ordinance, too, and, shortly after the motion passed, launched a counter-campaign to repeal the ban. The San Francisco city council did not properly weigh the "facts and a balancing of benefits with appropriate safeguards to restrain the technology's misuse," argued the

International Biometrics + Identity Association, which is headquartered in Washington, DC.[18]

A coalition of eight residents associations of San Francisco – under the banner Stop Crime SF – also called on the Board of Supervisors to amend the ordinance to allow at least some scope for facial recognition technology to protect their communities.[19] At the same time, Stop Crime SF began lobbying the city council to replace the ban with a moratorium. The residents want the city to regulate – not ban – the technology, arguing facial recognition can help locate missing persons, find lost adults with dementia, combat sex trafficking, and keep neighborhoods safe. "Let's keep the door open for when the technology improves," argues Joel Engardio, the vice-president of Stop Crime SF. "I'm not a fan of banning things when eventually it could actually be helpful."[20]

THE POLITICS OF BANS IN THE UNITED STATES

So far, San Francisco's ban on facial recognition technology has held up. And many other municipalities in the United States have followed suit with similar ordinances, including, among others, Alameda, Berkeley, and Oakland in California, Boston, Brookline, Cambridge, Easthampton, Northampton, Somerville, and Springfield in Massachusetts, and Portland in Maine.

In January 2020, for instance, the Cambridge City Council voted 9–0 to ban city officials from using facial recognition technology or accessing any information from such technology.[21] As in San Francisco, some did lobby against a full ban for policing, but to no avail. "I have tremendous faith in our police commissioner and our police department, but we have seen how facial recognition has been misused by governments," said Cambridge City councilor Marc McGovern when justifying the need to ban the technology in the city of Cambridge.[22] Kade Crockford, a director with the ACLU of Massachusetts, praised the Cambridge City Council. "Massachusetts cities and towns are stepping up to ensure that face surveillance technology doesn't get out ahead of our basic rights," she lauded. "We are particularly grateful for Cambridge's leadership on this issue, as a technology hub home to many tech workers and companies."[23]

In another milestone, in August 2020, Jackson, the capital of Mississippi, became the first city beyond the East and West coasts of the United States to ban its police department from using facial recognition technology. "We want the government solving crimes," said Councilor De'Keither Stamps, who backed the resolution. But we do not want one "tracking us, our whereabouts, where we go, how far we go, all day long."[24] The following month, as mentioned at the beginning of Chapter 3, the city of Portland in Oregon went even further, not only banning city officials from using FRT, but also, as of 2021, banning private businesses from deploying it in public spaces.

State legislatures are reining in facial recognition technology, too. California, New Hampshire, and Oregon have banned the use of facial recognition in police body cameras. Ohio has limited the use of facial recognition software by its police forces. Washington State is regulating how and when state officials can deploy face surveillance technology. Illinois and Texas require the consent of individuals to collect facial data legally. And Vermont has barred law enforcement officers from using FRT, except within the constraints of the regulated deployment of police drones. "By enacting the broadest outright ban on police use of facial recognition in the country, Vermont has taken the lead in protecting residents' civil liberties from this invasive and inaccurate technology," extoled Falko Schilling of the ACLU of Vermont.[25]

The recent history of facial recognition legislation in Massachusetts gives a sense of the contentious and shifting politics of campaigns for statewide bans in the United States. Over the past few years, community activists, researchers, and teachers in Massachusetts have been lobbying hard for laws to rein in the technology. State officials have been using the technology since at least 2006, without any regulatory oversight.[26] To spur state legislators to impose controls, in recent years activists have been filing lawsuits, campaigning on social media, and supporting municipal bans and moratoriums on facial recognition: a technology the ACLU of Massachusetts describes as "flawed" and "dangerous."[27] In addition, those opposing FRT have found allies within the Massachusetts Legislature, such as Democratic Senator Cynthia Creem who sponsored a 2019 bill that, if it had become law, would have imposed a moratorium on government use of facial recognition technology in Massachusetts.[28] "I personally don't want Big Sister watching me unless there are some rules, unless I know that it's effective, that it works, that it's doing its job and that it's being regulated," Senator Creem said. "None of that is happening right now."[29]

The 2019 facial recognition bill hit a wall of opposition. Republicans in the Massachusetts House and Senate pushed back. So did some Democrats. The Republican governor of Massachusetts, Charlie Baker, opposed the bill, as did police unions, biometrics firms, and trade associations. The trade association NetChoice – which includes Amazon,

Google, Twitter, and Facebook – lobbied against the legislation, as did the International Biometrics + Identity Association and the Security Industry Association.

The bill would "handcuff law enforcement from dealing with modern threats to public safety with modern tools," claimed NetChoice in a petition to the Massachusetts State Legislature.[30] The bill is "deeply flawed," and the "rush to ban" the "beneficial technology is unjustified," argued the Security Industry Association during testimony before a Massachusetts legislative committee.[31] Facial recognition technology is "essential to ensuring public safety, now and in the future," wrote the International Biometrics + Identity Association in a submission to the Massachusetts Legislature.[32]

Calls for a statewide moratorium on facial recognition technology, however, grew louder as Massachusetts legislators began to negotiate a police reform bill following the police murder of George Floyd in May 2020. Once again, though, supporters of facial recognition technology pushed back, emphasizing its potential value for identifying victims, solving crimes, and preventing terrorist attacks. "As much as facial recognition could be abused, it can also be used to save lives and exonerate the innocent," argued Republican Senator Bruce Tarr on the Massachusetts Senate floor. "Establishing a committee to study the technology, that makes sense," said Mark Leahy, executive director of the Massachusetts Chiefs of Police Association. "But to ban its use seems like another dramatic overreach."[33]

After months of wrangling, legislators did manage to reach a compromise. In December 2020, the Massachusetts House and Senate passed a 179-page police reform bill with a provision imposing a near-total ban on state officials or agencies using facial recognition technology until at least the end of 2021 (during which time a special commission would study the issue and recommend regulatory measures).[34] Under the bill, staff at the Massachusetts Registry of Motor Vehicles could continue to verify identities with facial recognition software before issuing licenses and permits (to prevent identify fraud). In an emergency or to execute a warrant for violent crimes, police could also ask the Registry of Motor Vehicles to conduct a facial recognition search of the motor vehicle database. These exceptions, however, did little to appease supporters of facial recognition software, who argued the bill effectively banned the technology for criminal investigations and crime prevention.

Significantly, the 2020 police reform bill did not have a veto-proof majority, having fractured the Democrats who held solid majorities in the Massachusetts House and Senate. Governor Baker sent the bill back to the Massachusetts Legislature, demanding, among other changes, the deletion of the provision severely limiting the use of facial recognition. "I'm not going to sign something that is going to ban facial recognition," Governor Baker told the *Boston Globe* newspaper. His reason was simple: a ban "ignores the important role it can play in solving crime."[35]

Governor Baker's demand for revisions ignited a firestorm of protest. Ayanna Pressley, a Democrat who serves the 7th district of Massachusetts in the US House of Representatives, called on the Massachusetts House and Senate to reject Governor Baker's proposed amendments.[36] The ACLU of Massachusetts urged the Massachusetts Legislature to "stand firm" against Governor Baker.[37] The entire roster of basketball players for the Boston Celtics penned an op-ed in the *Boston Globe* calling upon the Massachusetts Legislature and Governor Baker to retain the bill's strict controls on facial recognition technology. "By prohibiting government agencies from using face recognition technology to surveil people," the players wrote, "it will prevent racially-biased, discriminatory surveillance technology from being used to track us everywhere we go."[38]

Following intense negotiations, on December 31, 2020, Governor Baker signed an amended police reform bill into law. The revised bill retained the clause setting up a commission to study and recommend additional regulatory measures by the end of 2021. (The commission missed this deadline, but did issue its recommendations in March 2022.) Compared to the original version of the bill, however, the amended one gave the police far more leeway to use facial recognition technology to investigate crimes or avert a "substantial risk of harm."[39] "What we put on the governor's desk (originally) was a full ban of facial recognition techniques," explained Massachusetts Senator William Brownsberger. The revised bill "is a partial ban, or a limit, a regulation of them, and a study to explore the need for full regulation."[40]

This compromise disappointed those wanting an outright ban on the use of facial recognition technology for surveillance and routine policing. The legislation is "an improvement over the status quo, but stops well short of our goals," ACLU activists concluded.[41] Still, the fight to ban facial recognition technology in Massachusetts is far from over. For many, moreover, the added restrictions on the technology, and the police reforms more generally, were a notable victory for civil rights and civil liberties. Carlos González, a Democrat in the Massachusetts House who chairs the Black and Latino Caucus, praised Governor Baker's signing of the amended police reform bill. "Today begins to address decades of demands to bring reform and accountability to law enforcement institutions," he said. "The landmark legislation passed by the legislature and the governor begins to address the historic negative interactions between people of color and the police," added Sergeant Eddy Chrispin, president of the Massachusetts Association of Minority Law Enforcement Officers.[42]

The politics of facial recognition bans has been equally contentious within the US Congress. There is, as of 2022, no federal law in place to regulate facial recognition technology, although Democrats in the House and Senate did introduce a bill in 2020 that, while never having much chance of passing, would have halted the use of the technology by federal law enforcement and prevented states and municipal authorities from purchasing the technology with federal funds.[43] "The federal government must ban facial recognition until we have confidence that it doesn't exacerbate racism and violate the privacy of American citizens," said Democratic Senator Jeff Merkley. "Facial recognition technology doesn't just pose a grave threat to our privacy, it physically endangers Black Americans and other minority populations in our country," argued Democratic Senator Edward J. Markey. "Black and brown people are already over-surveilled and over-policed, and it's critical that we prevent government agencies from using this faulty technology to surveil communities of color even further," added Democratic Representative Ayanna Pressley.[44]

Activist organizations from across the United States endorsed this legislation. It is a "critical step toward a society where our communities can live without surveillance," said Brandi Collins-Dexter of Color of Change, a civil rights advocacy organization. "It's past time Congress halted the use of face recognition and stopped federal money from being used to invest in invasive and discriminatory surveillance," said the ACLU's Neema Singh Guliani when backing the legislation. It "effectively bans law enforcement use of facial recognition in the United States," said Evan Greer of Fight for the Future. "That's exactly what we need right now."[45]

Scores of other civil society groups are also now calling on the US Congress to suspend sales of facial recognition technology to US government agencies as well as do more to protect the privacy of facial data. Alongside, organizations such as the AI Now Institute at New York University are advocating for national laws to guarantee the right of communities to evaluate – and, if they want, reject – any public or private uses of facial recognition. The Institute is further calling for greater transparency and a "high threshold" of consent from individuals before firms or governments can use the technology. In the case of the United States, the Institute is calling for a moratorium on facial recognition technology "in sensitive social and political contexts" – such as for policing, surveillance, hiring, and public education – until exacting regulatory measures are put in place, including stricter biometric privacy laws.[46]

The AI Now Institute has particular concerns with the accuracy and value of affect recognition technology, which infers feelings, intent, emotions, political orientation, personality, and mental states by analyzing personal features such as facial expressions, gestures, gait, and voice. The claims of this technology, the AI Now Institute argues, "are not backed by robust scientific evidence," and surreptitiously using it to evaluate job candidates, judge insurance claims, and interrogate suspects "creates deeply concerning risks, at both an individual and societal level."[47] The AI Now Institute has called upon US lawmakers to ban affect recognition technology for any significant decision-making, including hiring, sentencing, policing, medical assessments, and evaluating educational performance.

Privacy, civil rights, social justice, and civil liberties campaigners are also pressuring firms to not sell face surveillance products to governments.[48] Employees, shareholders, and consumers have increased the pressure on some firms. One leading company to agree is Google, which, following its Artificial Intelligence Principles, has never sold these products, and has said it has no plans to do so.[49] Another company to agree is IBM, which, after shelving its general-purpose facial recognition software in 2020, then called on the US Commerce Department to impose strict controls on the export of face surveillance technology to countries with "a history of human rights abuses."[50]

Yet another company to agree is Axon, the largest supplier of police body cameras in the United States. In 2019, Axon pledged to not integrate facial recognition software into its products – at least for now – saying the technology was too unreliable and "could exacerbate existing inequities in policing."[51] This came after a coalition of more than 40 privacy, justice, and civil rights groups called upon Axon to "not offer or enable" any "real-time face recognition analysis of live video captured by body-worn cameras," arguing this would further entrench racialized policing and have a deeply chilling effect on freedom of speech and the constitutional right to dissent and protest.[52]

FACIAL RECOGNITION CREEP IN THE UNITED STATES

The movement against facial recognition technology does seem to be strengthening across the United States. Both Republicans and Democrats in the US Congress have voiced concerns. Still, campaigners have had far less influence on the national stage than in cities such as San Francisco. At the time of writing in 2022, Congress had done little to control facial recognition technology, and polls continue to find solid support for facial recognition technology among some voters.[53] Airports, schools, prisons, and stores are installing the technology. American technology firms, meanwhile, are continuing to develop and sell facial recognition products – such as the Pasadena-based company Wolfcom, which in 2020 was beta testing live facial recognition body cameras for US law enforcement.[54]

Hundreds of federal, state, and local police forces across the United States would appear to be using facial recognition technology. Much of this is done quietly or in secrecy, and the full extent of use by police departments and intelligence agencies is unclear. We do know the Federal Bureau of Investigation (FBI) has been using facial recognition to identify suspects within databases of driver licenses and identification photos.[55] We know that US Immigration and Customs Enforcement has been using facial recognition technology to search state driver-license databases. We know the US Drug Enforcement Administration has piloted Microsoft's facial recognition software. And we know that US Customs and Border Protection is using facial recognition technology to identify travelers in airports and seaports. Seeing this, at the end of 2021 Senator Ed Markey concluded: "Facial recognition technology is metastasizing throughout the federal government."[56]

At least 30 states also allow local police and authorities to search driver-license databases with facial recognition software. Some are doing so more responsibly than others. "A few agencies have instituted meaningful protections to prevent the misuse of the technology," notes one investigative report for the Center on Privacy & Technology at Georgetown Law. "In many more cases, it is out of control."[57]

Even a quick glance, then, shows the technology is continuing to spread across police departments, federal agencies, schools, and private businesses across the United States. As we will see next, the politics of facial recognition regulation in the state of Washington, and more broadly in the rest of the United States, offers revealing insights into why.

5. Regulating facial recognition in the United States

Elected in 2019, Joe Nguyen is the first Washington State Senator of Vietnamese descent, and the first person of color to represent the 34th district of the Washington Senate. The son of refugees from Vietnam, he has much to be proud of. As a boy, he lived in public housing, helping to care for his father who was left a quadriplegic after a car accident, and working as a janitor at his own high school to help support his family. Even as a young man, he was a natural leader, serving three times as class president of his high school and two times as president of the student body at Seattle University.

Since graduating from Seattle University in 2006, he has worked hard to give back to his community, volunteering in homeless shelters and sitting on a community advisory committee to promote just and fair policing. Running as a Democrat, he won his Senate seat pledging to advance social justice, reduce inequality, tackle systemic racism, and improve the lives of his constituents, especially those struggling at the margins of society. And in his first year he helped the Democrats pass progressive bills to increase spending on mental health and education and support clean-energy technologies.[1]

SENATOR NGUYEN'S FACIAL RECOGNITION LAW

In early 2020, Senator Nguyen sponsored a bill to regulate the use of facial recognition technology by police and government agencies. "The companies that are already producing this technology don't care about the moral implications involved – they care about profit," Nguyen said as he strove to get the backing to pass his bill. "That's why we need to take action now to hold these companies accountable and ensure that public agencies don't keep using this technology without any regulatory checks or balances."[2]

In the end, his bill passed the Washington State House of Representatives by a vote of 53 to 43 and the Washington State Senate by a vote of 27 to 21, and, on March 31, 2020, Governor Jay Inslee signed it into law (in effect from July 2021). "Right now, we have seen this technology already being used without much concern for the moral implications that are associated with it," said Senator Nguyen after Governor Inslee approved the legislation. "This bill will change that, and ensure that facial recognition isn't being used unless there are regulatory checks and balances."[3]

The legislation requires authorities to obtain a warrant to use facial recognition technology for "ongoing surveillance," "real-time or near real-time identification," or "persistent tracking." Police can only use it to investigate serious crimes – or in an emergency such as a Silver or Amber alert – and must disclose its use to defendants before trial. Police are not allowed to use the technology to monitor or investigate a person's involvement in a "noncriminal organization or lawful event." Nor can authorities base a warrant or court order on "religious, political or social views or activities" or "actual or perceived race, ethnicity, citizenship, place of origin, immigration status, age, disability, gender, gender identity, sexual orientation, or other characteristic protected by law."[4]

Any facial recognition software used by authorities, meanwhile, must undergo independent testing to evaluate its accuracy and check for racial, gender, and age biases. In addition, agencies must develop a data management policy, meet accountability standards, and give public notice of intent before using the technology. Staff using facial recognition software are also required to undergo training to promote "meaningful human" oversight of the technology.[5]

A MODEL BILL?

Many of those advocating for regulation of facial recognition technology (rather than bans) see ways to strengthen the legislation in Washington State. Still, most advocates of regulation agree it is a praiseworthy compromise. "These rules are promising, but there will certainly be loopholes exploited by the slippery lawyers of Silicon Valley," argues tech reporter Jamie Davies. "However, Washington State legislators should be applauded for their efforts to control a potentially divisive technology."[6]

Some advocates of regulation are going even further, hailing the bill as a pathbreaking model for the world. The Microsoft Corporation, which lobbied hard for its passage, has been leading the applause. The president of Microsoft, Brad Smith, publicly thanked Senator Nguyen for steering the bill through the legislature, and wrote: Its "balanced approach ensures that facial recognition can be used as a tool to protect the public, but only in ways that respect fundamental rights and serve the public interest."[7]

Others, though, think the bill sets a dangerous precedent, paving the way for the normalization of facial recognition technology for policing and surveillance in the United States. It is telling, the critics note, that the architect of Washington State's facial recognition bill – Senator Nguyen – is a Microsoft employee, and has been since 2013.[8]

THE POLITICS OF MICROSOFT

Microsoft first began to lobby openly for facial recognition regulations a few years ago. It is essential to develop "thoughtful government regulation" and "norms around acceptable uses" of facial recognition technology, Brad Smith wrote on the company's official blog in 2018.[9]

Why, you might wonder, is Microsoft so keen to see states like Washington regulate facial recognition technology? In part, the company is aiming to protect its brand value and project an image of social responsibility. It is partly reacting to pressure from employees to follow the company's self-declared ethical principles for governing artificial intelligence.[10] And it is partly responding to the need to retain – and recruit – the world's most talented AI software engineers, who are in short supply and heavy demand as artificial intelligence enriches businesses around the world.[11]

The biggest reason Microsoft has been lobbying for regulations, however, is to enhance its ability to compete profitably in the growing global market for facial recognition products – from authorizing building access to verifying ticket holders to automating public transportation to watching for shoplifters. The company is also keen to sell facial recognition products to law enforcement agencies, including American police departments once US national regulations are in place. "Responsible" firms like Microsoft should not "cede" this market to unethical companies, Brad Smith said in defense of these plans.[12]

Microsoft wants to create a playing field with less risk to its brand value and more potential for profits, not just in the US, but worldwide. By shaping regulatory rulebooks, Microsoft is trying to corral startups that are profiting from low standards. It is aiming to rein in American competitors. It is looking to gain an edge over competitors from Japan (such as NEC) and Europe (such as Gemalto headquartered in Amsterdam and Idemia headquartered in Paris). It is hoping to weaken firms with innate advantages in lawless markets, such as those from China and Russia. And it is aiming to avoid bans.

"Many facial recognition debates, including one that took place last year in Washington State itself, have foundered in gridlock over whether to ban this new technology," Brad Smith wrote just after Governor Inslee signed Washington State's facial recognition law. "But, as this new law so clearly illustrates, there is so much to be gained from more thorough consideration of ways to protect the public from the risks of facial recognition by regulating its beneficial use."[13]

DENOUNCING WASHINGTON STATE'S FACIAL RECOGNITION REGULATION

Many civil rights, civil liberty, and social justice organizations disagree vehemently with Brad Smith's assessment. The legislation "purports to put safeguards around the use of facial recognition technology, but does just the opposite," argues Jennifer Lee, a project manager for the ACLU of Washington. It allows, as she reads it, facial recognition surveillance of "entire crowds at football stadiums, places of worship, or on public street corners, chilling people's constitutionally protected rights and civil liberties."[14]

There is, Lee contends, no community oversight, weak accountability mechanisms, and insufficient human oversight. Nor does the law contain any specific enforcement instrument. In her view, when all is said and done, the legislation dangerously extends the policing and surveillance powers of state authorities. She is calling for an immediate halt to using the technology in Washington State to allow marginalized communities – and not police departments and technology companies – to determine whether it "should be used at all."[15]

Tech journalist Dave Gershgorn also thinks the new law has deep "flaws," doing very little to constrain the government's ability to use the technology for routine policing and crowd surveillance, and doing nothing at all to rein in sales to police departments or hold companies accountable for identification errors. Gershgorn is especially concerned with what he thinks is a major loophole in the legislation: when "exigent circumstances exist," authorities can still conduct real-time and ongoing surveillance without a warrant.[16]

Similarly, tech journalist Mehreen Kasana describes the legislation as "sketchy." It may look reasonable, but in her view grave threats to civil society lurk below the surface. It is naïve, she argues, to assume that any regulation can control facial recognition technology – and it is downright malicious, as Brad Smith is doing, to claim that a law as weak as Washington State's is ever going to stop authorities from abusing it.[17]

THE POLITICS OF REGULATION IN THE UNITED STATES

Similar bills have been introduced in other state legislatures, such as California, South Dakota, Maryland, and Idaho, with some passages identical to ones in the Washington State legislation. The bill introduced by Republican Britt Raybould to the Idaho House of Representatives, for instance, was based on a draft of the Washington State bill that Microsoft sent her. "It's a starting point," she said of her bill.[18]

Microsoft is continuing to lobby for regulation, describing, for example, the proposed facial recognition legislation in California in 2020 as "a thoughtful approach which recognizes the need for safeguards to balance the opportunities and the risks associated with facial recognition technology."[19] Numerous privacy and civil liberties organizations, however, opposed the California State legislation. So did many civil rights and social justice organizations, such as the California Immigrant Policy Center and the California chapters of the NAACP.

Critics argued the 2020 California State legislation, which failed to pass, would normalize the use of facial recognition technology for policing and surveillance. "We should not be giving companies and governments a green light to use facial recognition to track individuals, deny economic opportunities, and further marginalize communities," argued a coalition of more than 40 activist organizations in a submission to state legislators.[20] Legal scholars, medical professionals, and other academics also opposed the California State legislation, with one group arguing in a letter to the bill's sponsor, Ed Chau: The "bill threatens to further entrench inequity and divert money from vital public health resources while ushering in a nightmarish future of unprecedented biometric surveillance."[21]

Such resistance is delaying and blocking facial recognition legislation across the United States. Still, those advocating for regulation do seem to be gaining ground. Nonprofit organizations such as the Information Technology and Innovation Foundation are backing calls for facial recognition regulations for policing, public surveillance, and private businesses.[22] Experts are voicing support. So are community groups. And, most significantly, technology companies are ramping up lobbying efforts, at both state and national levels. "Tech giants are spending tens of millions of dollars to stave off real reforms and – even worse – push legislation that would repeal local facial recognition bans," claims Albert Fox Cahn of the Surveillance Technology Oversight Project (S.T.O.P), which opposes mass surveillance and litigates for privacy rights.[23]

As it has been doing in the state of Massachusetts since 2019, for instance, the trade association NetChoice has been petitioning legislators to reject calls to ban or severely restrict facial recognition technology. "Every day facial recognition technologies help law enforcement to generate leads in cases, such as homicide, rape, armed robbery and other violent crime, as well as identifying elderly persons stricken with dementia, finding lost and missing children, identifying homeless persons with mental illness and identifying deceased persons," contends Carl Szabo, the vice president of NetChoice.[24]

Other industry groups are arguing along the same lines. In a 2019 letter to US congressional leaders in the House and Senate, one coalition of industry organizations and trade associations claims "a moratorium on the use of FRT would be premature and have unintended consequences not only for innovation, safety and security but for the continued improvement of the technology's accuracy and effectiveness." Instead, "we all agree that the technology should be used carefully with proper guardrails balancing privacy and civil liberties considerations."[25] The coalition of trade associations, business groups, and facial recognition developers, retailers, and users also set up a working group of core firms to develop policy recommendations for legislators. "We're not opposed to regulation, but we oppose a ban," emphasized Tim Day, a senior vice-president at the US Chamber of Commerce, which convened the working group.[26]

Similarly, Amazon, like Microsoft, is now openly pressing for industry-friendly national regulation. Michael Punke, a vice-president at Amazon Web Services (AWS), argues the technology "is an important, even critical, tool for business, government, and law enforcement use." He does accept that the technology brings risks, which explains why, he says, his company supports developing "an appropriate national legislative framework that protects individual civil rights," while simultaneously "allowing for continued innovation and practical application of the technology."[27]

That said, for years after its launch in 2016 Amazon shrugged off demands to shelve its cloud-based face recognition service known as Rekognition, which has the capacity to identify faces in real time. "We demand that Amazon stop powering a government surveillance infra-structure that poses a grave threat to customers and communities across the country," more than 60 advocacy organizations wrote in 2018 in an open letter to Amazon's Jeff Bezos.[28]

In the wake of the May 2020 murder of George Floyd by Minneapolis police, however, and facing mounting pressure from shareholders, Amazon did promise in June 2020 to stop selling US police access to Rekognition for a year. "We hope this one-year moratorium," Amazon posted on its website, "might give Congress enough time to implement appropriate rules, and we stand ready to help if requested."[29]

Some civil society campaigners praised Amazon's move as a step in the right direction, especially after Amazon extended the moratorium in 2021 "until further notice."[30] But others were critical, wanting Amazon to commit to stop developing and selling facial recognition or analysis software (as IBM did in 2020), and seeing the moratorium as yet another crafty maneuver to pave the way for the normalization of facial recognition technology for policing, state surveillance, and school security.

Jimmy Gomez, a Democrat in the US House of Representatives and a member of the House Committee on Oversight and Reform, captured this sentiment well in a letter to Jeff Bezos in response to Amazon's announcement. "After two years of formal congressional inquiries – including bicameral letters, House Oversight Committee hearings, and in-person meetings – Amazon has yet to adequately address questions about the dangers its facial recognition technology can pose to privacy and civil rights, the accuracy of the technology, and its disproportionate impact on communities of color," he wrote. "Corporations have been quick to share expressions of support for the Black Lives Matter move-ment following the public outrage over the murders of Black Americans like George Floyd at the hands of police. Unfortunately, too many of these gestures have been performative at best. Calling on Congress to regulate facial recognition technology is one of these gestures."[31]

The day after Amazon's pledge, Microsoft declared it would not sell any facial recognition technology to US police forces until Congress passed a national law to regulate the technology.[32] Like with Amazon's pledge, however, this promise did little to reassure the civil rights, privacy rights, and civil liberties organizations that see industry-friendly regulation – such as Senator Nguyen's bill in Washington State – as a beachhead for even greater surveillance and heavy-handed, racist policing.[33]

Microsoft's pledge "should feel like winning, but it feels more like a thinly veiled threat," said Liz O'Sullivan, a member of S.T.O.P.'s community advisory board. Jameson Spivack, a researcher at Georgetown University's Law Center, is equally wary of Microsoft. The company, he said, is lobbying for legislation that may look strict at first glance, but which, in reality, does very little to control the technology. "It's their way of getting ahead of the opposition and coopting the movement," he concluded.[34]

Growing resistance to facial recognition technology is influencing the political landscape of the United States. It is persuading some municipalities to ban the technology. It is derailing industry-backed FRT legislation. It is pushing some government agencies, such as the Internal Revenue Service in 2022, to shelve plans to require facial authentication to access online accounts and services. It is convincing companies such as Amazon and Microsoft to hold back on selling the technology to US police departments. It is inducing US concert promoters and colleges to promise to forgo the technology. And, to forestall or override strict controls or bans, it is spurring technology firms, the airline industry, retailers, and the security industry to push even harder for market-friendly rules across the United States, including lobbying the US Congress and the administration of President Joe Biden to pass federal legislation allowing for regulated use of the technology.[35] Local resistance to FRT is growing in other countries too, although, as I explore next, this resistance is not influencing local civic politics nearly as much, especially in low-income countries, authoritarian regimes, and democracies with less priority on civil liberties, personal freedoms, and privacy rights.

6. Rising global opposition to face surveillance

Headquartered in San Francisco, the Electronic Frontier Foundation is an international nonprofit that combines policy analysis, litigation, technological innovation, and community activism to advocate for digital rights, freedoms, and privacy. In October 2019, in Tirana, Albania, it joined more than 100 civil society organizations to issue the Albania Declaration, which calls on all "countries to suspend the further deployment of facial recognition technology for mass surveillance."[1] A month later the Electronic Frontier Foundation launched "About Face," a grassroots campaign to offer a "model bill" to help US legislators ban face surveillance, which it defines as "an automated or semi-automated process that assists in identifying or verifying an individual, or captures information about them, based on the physical characteristics of their face."[2]

Katitza Rodriguez is the Policy Director for Global Privacy at the Electronic Frontier Foundation. She sees 2019 as a turning point in the global campaign to stop police, intelligence services, schools, and private businesses from deploying face surveillance technology. "Activists took action against face recognition in countries all over the world," she wrote in a review of the year.[3] The Covid-19 pandemic did end up derailing the global campaign in the first half of 2020. But calls to ban face surveillance resurged following the May 2020 murder of George Floyd by Minneapolis police officers, with activists all over the world pointing to facial recognition technology as an example of a racist policing tool.

The "global fight" to end face surveillance, as Rodriguez predicted, would indeed appear to be gaining momentum.[4] Yet great care is necessary to avoid exaggerating the movement's worldwide power, as some observers are doing. The intensity of the local civic politics opposing face surveillance, we need to keep in mind, varies widely across the world. On a general level, as this chapter will elaborate further, the layers of civil society resistance run deepest in Western democracies, and tend to be shallow in impoverished states, repressive regimes, and political cultures that prioritize social harmony, community responsibility, and respect for authority.

UNEVEN RESISTANCE TO FACE SURVEILLANCE

Looking at the country headquarters of the 112 organizations signing the Albania Declaration offers a sense of the uneven character of the transnational social movement opposing face surveillance. More than two-thirds of the signatories are located in European and North American democracies where citizens have relatively strong civil liberties and political rights – what the nonprofit organization Freedom House describes as "free." Only 12 percent are based in countries that Freedom House considers "partly free" (6 percent) or "not free" (6 percent).[5] Organizations with headquarters in the United States and the United Kingdom alone account for 40 percent of all signatories. Ones from the Asia-Pacific region account for just 7 percent of the total, while ones from Africa comprise a mere 3 percent. No organization from China signed the declaration.[6]

Looking inside countries and regions confirms the wide variation in the depth of resistance. A coalition of over 85 groups in the United States signed letters in 2019 calling on Amazon and Microsoft to commit to not selling face surveillance products to governments.[7] In less than a week at the beginning of the 2020 school year in the United States, more than 1,000 parents across 50 states signed an open letter by Fight for the Future calling for an "outright ban on facial recognition" in American schools.[8] More than 60 groups, meanwhile, have joined with the American Civil Liberties Union to campaign across the United States for laws to ban the use of facial recognition technology for policing and surveillance.[9]

At the same time, over 30 groups in Canada are calling on the federal government to ban the use of face surveillance technology by national law enforcement agencies.[10] In Europe, a network of 44 civil society groups – under the banner of the European Digital Rights network – has called on authorities within the European Union to "comprehensively and indefinitely" ban public face surveillance "in both law and practice."[11] To push for such a ban, a coalition of activist groups is coordinating under the slogan "Reclaim Your Face," with targeted campaigns in countries such as the Czech Republic, France, Italy, Germany, Greece, the Netherlands, Serbia, and Slovenia.[12]

RESISTING FACE SURVEILLANCE IN EUROPE

Civil society opposition to face surveillance is growing inside just about every European country. In the United Kingdom, a coalition of 25 NGOs – including Amnesty International, Big Brother Watch, Liberty, the Institute of Race Relations, the Open Rights Group, and Privacy International – is calling on the UK government to ban the use of live facial recognition by police forces and businesses.[13] Some of these groups, such as Big Brother Watch and Liberty, have gone to court to try to prevent police and security forces from using live facial recognition. Researchers at institutes and universities in the UK are also raising awareness and educating the general public.[14]

The Equality and Human Rights Commission (EHRC) – an independent, regulatory body responsible for advancing equality, protecting human rights, and preventing discrimination in England, Scotland, and Wales – has voiced concerns too, calling for a moratorium on face surveillance technology until appropriate legal controls are in place.[15] Parliamentary inquiries have reached similar conclusions. A justice subcommittee of the Scottish Parliament, for instance, concluded in 2020 that live facial recognition technology was a threat to privacy and human rights, and that deployment by Police Scotland would violate the "principle of policing by consent."[16] Convener John Finnie of the Scottish Green Party explains where his committee landed after reviewing the evidence: "So whether this technology is being used by private companies, public authorities or the police, the Scottish government needs to ensure there is a clear legal framework to protect the public and police alike from operating in a facial recognition Wild West."[17]

In France, more than 80 civil society organizations have called on the French parliament to ban – "now and in the future" – the use of facial recognition for surveillance or security purposes. "Facial recognition is a uniquely invasive and dehumanizing technology," the coalition wrote in an open letter, "which makes possible, sooner or later, constant surveillance of the public space."[18] Similar demands, critiques, and alliances are emerging across Europe, as in Germany with the "Face Recognition Stop" coalition, to name just one example.[19]

Opposition to facial recognition is even growing in Russia, a country Freedom House labels as "not free." Russia's digital rights NGO Roskomsvoboda, for instance, has launched a campaign calling for a moratorium on facial recognition technology for mass surveillance.

The spread of this technology across Russia, Roskomsvoboda is arguing, threatens civil society by chilling dissent and protest, collecting data without affirmative consent, and contributing to violations of citizen rights by security forces and corporations.[20]

In response to growing criticism, a few European states have begun to rein in facial recognition technology. In 2019, the Swedish Data Protection Authority fined a high school for trialing the technology to take attendance, although later that year it did authorize its use for policing after concluding that data protections were sufficient.[21] In Belgium, the Supervisory Body for Police Information – an independent parliamentary body – ruled in 2019 that a pilot project to use facial recognition for screening at Brussels Airport did not comply with national policing and data privacy laws.[22] In Italy in 2020, the Italian Data Protection Authority forced the municipality of Como to turn off a Huawei facial recognition security system monitoring a public park next to the train station.[23]

In France in 2019, meanwhile, the Commission Nationale de l'Informatique et des Libertés (CNIL) – an independent regulatory body to support data privacy laws – advised that plans to install facial recognition technology in high schools in southern France would not be legal under the EU's General Data Protection Regulation, which came into force in 2018.[24] Privacy activists hailed the decision. Advocates for the project, meanwhile, were left shaking their heads. The decision was "a century late," said Renaud Muselie, the president of the Regional Council of Provence-Alpes-Côte d'Azur. "In a world where facial recognition is in the everyday life of millions of smartphone users," he bristled, "refusing projects as simple and ambitious as ours is baffling."[25]

Other EU laws and institutions have the potential to further restrain facial recognition technology across Europe. The EU Charter of Fundamental Rights guarantees "everyone" in the European Union "the right to the protection of personal data."[26] In 2020, the European Commission considered placing a 3–5 year moratorium on governments and corporations using facial recognition technology in public spaces and, although this option was ultimately rejected, since then the Commission has been encouraging member states to regulate facial recognition technology.[27] The European Union Agency for Fundamental Rights, meanwhile, has voiced concerns regarding live facial recognition technology, noting: "To prevent fundamental rights violations and effectively support those people whose fundamental rights are affected by facial recognition technology, oversight authorities must have sufficient powers, resources and expertise."[28]

The European Parliament, as Chapter 2 noted, did pass a nonbinding resolution in 2021 calling for a ban on facial recognition technology for predictive policing and public surveillance. To date, however, the vast majority of governments in Europe have either been giving the technology free rein or relying on a "patchwork" of privacy laws, human rights charters, data regulations, policing guidelines, court rulings, and the advice of public regulatory bodies.[29]

Kate Saslow, a project manager at the German think tank Stiftung Neue Verantwortung, describes FRT regulation in the EU as disjointed, perfunctory, and ambiguous, where rhetoric is far stronger than action – a "wild west" in comparison to the cities and states now regulating the technology in the United States. For her, this explains why corporate pledges to suspend sales of facial recognition technology to US police departments do not necessarily extend to Europe. It explains why local bans and strict rules for FRT are so rare inside European states. It explains why technology companies are setting Europe's technology agendas. And it explains why the technology is popping up all over the region.[30]

Some observers, though, see fewer differences between Europe and the United States. At the end of the day, argue tech journalists Janosch Delcker and Cristiano Lima, technology companies in both places remain "largely in control of where and how to deploy facial recognition."[31] Interestingly, this is less true across the developing world, not because of civil society resistance, but because governments are doing more to develop and deploy the technology as a tool for policing and mass surveillance.

RESISTING FACE SURVEILLANCE IN THE DEVELOPING WORLD

Civil society resistance to face surveillance technology is strengthening across the developing world too, although more slowly than in Europe and North America.[32] Organizations from countries such as India and Brazil are also assuming leadership roles in transnational advocacy campaigns. As Chapter 3 noted, of the six organizations drafting the 2021 open letter launching the worldwide campaign to "Ban Biometric Surveillance," one is from India (the Internet Freedom Foundation) and one is from Brazil (Instituto Brasileiro de Defesa do Consumidor). Of the 193 organizations signing this letter, over 40 percent are in developing countries in Asia, Africa, and Latin America, including 15 from India and 27 from Brazil. Looking at the signatories, moreover, reveals the growing opposition to face surveillance in repressive regimes, with 22 percent of signatories located in Asian, African, and Latin American countries that Freedom House considers "partly free" (18 percent) or "not free" (4 percent).[33]

Resistance in Brazil is growing in part because President Jair Bolsonaro, who came to power in 2019, is moving especially quickly to integrate facial recognition technology into policing and security services, telling the public that high-tech surveillance prevents murders and gang violence. Some Brazilian lawmakers have even pushed for national legislation to make facial recognition cameras mandatory in public areas.[34] A diverse array of local groups in Brazil, however, see the technology as a threat to civil liberties and human rights, and are calling on Brazilian authorities to stop using it to monitor favelas (shantytowns) and search crowds for wanted criminals.

Nonprofit groups within Brazil are working as well to try to stop firms from using FRT in public spaces to collect consumer data and tailor digital advertising. Arguing it violated data and consumer rights, for instance, in 2018 the Brazilian Institute for Consumer Protection got a court injunction to stop a private company from using facial analysis cameras to evaluate the age, gender, and reactions of people gazing at digital advertising on train doors in a subway in São Paulo.[35] As legal proceedings went forward, in 2020 Access Now prepared an "expert opinion," concluding: Those riding the subway were "subjected to invasive surveillance and judgement of their inner emotional life, and had no opportunity to opt out of or to deny consent to such processing of their data and did not receive clear information about the system."[36] Verónica Arroyo, a policy analyst at Access Now (Peru), is calling on the courts to ban the use of facial analysis technology in São Paulo's subway system, arguing it "sets a frightening precedent" for both Brazil and the world.[37]

Opposition to face surveillance technology is also rising in other developing countries. Four local organizations in Argentina had signed the Albania Declaration by 2022, and, as in Brazil, local NGOs are pursuing legal action to oppose face surveillance. One example is Argentina's Association for Civil Rights – the Asociación por los Derechos Civiles (ADC) – which has challenged the constitutionality of the live face surveillance system in place in train stations in Buenos Aires since 2019.[38] In Paraguay, meanwhile, the digital rights Association of Technology, Education, Development, Research and Communication (TEDIC) – the only NGO from this country to sign the Albania Declaration – has been filing lawsuits to obtain more information about facial recognition applications in the capital city, Asunción, including for the airport, bus stations, and downtown streets.[39]

Activists within India are pushing back, too.[40] Facial recognition technology is spreading steadily across India, including for policing and surveillance of public protests. The Internet Freedom Foundation, which advocates for digital rights and liberties, is taking legal action and filing information requests to try to stop police from using the technology for surveillance. "The use of the system for profiling and surveillance at public congregations is illegal and unconstitutional," argues Apar Gupta, the foundation's executive director.[41]

International advocacy organizations such as Amnesty International and Human Rights Watch are also raising awareness of the dangers of face surveillance technology for privacy, civil liberties, and human rights in the developing world, such as in Hyderabad city in India.[42] Amnesty International is campaigning for a worldwide ban on the "use, development, production, sale, and export of facial recognition technology for mass surveillance" by states.[43] This surveillance technology, argues Maya Wang of Human Rights Watch, poses an existential threat to privacy. "Privacy is a gateway right," she said. "Once you lose that, you basically lose all your rights."[44]

Still, even as the voices of opposition grow louder, few, if any, regulatory controls exist over facial recognition surveillance in the developing world. This is true in the BRICS – Brazil, Russia, India, China, and South Africa. And it is true across most of Africa, the Asia-Pacific, and Latin America. There are a few exceptions. From 2019 to the end of 2020, for instance, Morocco imposed a moratorium on facial recognition technology to give the government time to establish data management protocols.[45] But, across the vast majority of the developing world, governments are not reining in facial recognition technology, and are instead actively backing the technology to extend state powers over civil society.

As we've seen, a few jurisdictions in Western liberal democracies have banned or restricted facial recognition technology. And a few governments in the developing world are starting to regulate the use of the technology for policing and surveillance. What do these trends suggest for the future of facial recognition technology? Might it still be possible, as some activists are hoping, to "beat back" this technology?[46] To answer this question, it is necessary to better understand the political and economic forces underlying rising worldwide uptake: the theme of Part III.

PART III

The global political economy of facial recognition

7. The corporate politics of facial recognition

The world's best-known technology firms are at the core of the political economy of facial recognition technology. Microsoft and Amazon are openly lobbying for industry-friendly regulations. Apple, while staying away from the face surveillance market for policing, is competing hard to integrate facial verification and photo tagging into its products and services. China's big technology firms, such as Baidu, Alibaba, and Tencent, are embracing the technology with equal enthusiasm. Meanwhile, Japan's Panasonic and NEC corporations and France's Thales Group are quietly increasing sales of facial recognition technology for law enforcement, health, and retailing – a global market set to exceed US$16 billion by 2030, more than quadruple the value in 2020.[1]

Yet companies with far less brand recognition are a comparable, if not greater, force within this political economy. American biometrics software firms are major players in a market where numerous medium and small firms are competing fiercely. There are large numbers of AI and machine learning startups gaining market traction too, such as Russia's NtechLab. A long list of Chinese tech companies, meanwhile, are vying to install face surveillance systems both at home and abroad: ones such as Dahua, Hikvision, Huawei, iFlyTek, Jiadu Technology, Megvii, SenseTime, and Yitu. Small-time entrepreneurs are also playing an outsized role on the world stage. No one, though, has become quite as notorious as Hoan Ton-That, the CEO of Clearview AI, an American software startup.

THE STORY OF CLEARVIEW AI

Hoan Ton-That is your typical tech entrepreneur: bold, creative, and prone to spin. Dropping out of university in 2007, he left his home country of Australia at the age of 19 to make his fortune in San Francisco. There, he developed more than 20 apps, including one for pasting Donald Trump's yellow hair onto headshots. None were particularly successful.

He then worked for a time at AngelList – a fundraising platform for start-ups – before heading off to New York City in 2016.

Tall, with long jet-black hair, he tried his hand at modeling, but this did not work out. Then, by happenstance, he met Richard Schwartz, a conservative political operator who has worked for many well-connected bosses, including Rudy Giuliani, a former mayor of New York City and legal advisor to Donald Trump. Schwartz and Ton-That decided to launch a facial recognition startup, with Ton-That handling the logistics and Schwartz the financing.

The idea was simple: develop a facial recognition app able to identify a face and supply background information, not by searching a database of mugshots, licenses, or passport photos, as was already common, but by searching a database of internet images. Ton-That hired one software engineer to develop a facial recognition system from publicly available research and algorithms; he hired another to write a program to scrape facial images from websites, video platforms, and social media. Facebook, Twitter, and YouTube were all scraped. So were Instagram and LinkedIn and Flickr. Before long, he had a database of three billion facial images.

As 2017 drew to a close, Ton-That and his small team were nearly destitute. But, under a company registered as Smartcheckr, they were making progress on building a truly novel facial recognition product. At this point, though, Ton-That and Schwartz were still struggling to find a marketing angle. Having now received US$200,000 in backing from Peter Thiel, a billionaire venture capitalist who cofounded PayPal, they decided to rebrand the company as Clearview AI.[2]

By the middle of 2019, investors had poured millions of dollars into Clearview AI. By then, Ton-That and Schwartz had settled on a marketing strategy: license the facial recognition app to law enforcement and private businesses. Mobilizing Schwartz's network, they talked up the app within right-wing circles as a way of identifying neighborhood criminals and illegal immigrants. They also offered free trials and discounted rates to police departments, intelligence agencies, and the security divisions of private businesses.[3]

Promotional emails were sent to rank-and-file officers describing the app as a "Google search for faces," promising "unlimited searches," and urging them "to run wild with your searches."[4] Before long, staff at the US Department of Justice, the FBI, Homeland Security, the US Drug Enforcement Administration, US Immigration and Customs Enforcement, the US Secret Service, and hundreds of police departments across the United States had all tried the technology. So had law enforcement investigators across Canada, including within the RCMP. So had police and intelligence analysts in Australia, Brazil, and the United Arab Emirates, as well as more than a dozen countries of Europe. And so had officers at the International Criminal Police Organization, better known as Interpol.[5]

Easy to use, officers were uploading video stills and photos to identify suspects, victims, and witnesses, as well as obtain links to online information about the person. "With Clearview, you can use photos that aren't perfect," Nick Ferrara, a detective in Gainesville, Florida, told the *New York Times*. "A person can be wearing a hat or glasses, or it can be a profile shot or partial view of their face."[6] Other detectives and police officers were equally impressed with the performance of the Clearview app. Yet most law enforcement officials did not understand how the technology actually worked. Nor, as 2019 drew to a close, did anyone know much about the company behind the technology.

By now, *New York Times* reporter Kashmir Hill was on the hunt to learn more about Clearview AI. When she first began investigating in November 2019, she struggled to uncover even basic information about the company. Clearview AI's website was barebones, with a fake address in Manhattan as its headquarters. No one who she thought might work for the company returned her calls or emails. LinkedIn uncovered just one employee: a sales manager named John Good, who, she would later discover, was an alias for none other than Hoan Ton-That.

She did get the sense that her persistence was jangling nerves. To better understand the capabilities of the Clearview app, she'd asked her contacts in the New York Police Department to upload her photo to see what images and information came up. Soon, Clearview staff were phoning the officers to ask if they had been talking with the media about the company. Did this mean, she wondered, that Clearview staff could see who the police were searching for?

Not long afterward, Ton-That began to respond to some of Hill's queries. The Clearview app was not designed to gather evidence for prosecutions, he said, but was simply a tool to help a detective investigate crimes or generate leads in a cold case. He was hiding nothing, he added. His company was merely in stealth mode, a common startup strategy to avoid alerting competitors. His staff did not track police searches, he insisted. To prevent "inappropriate searches," he said, the AI system "flags possible anomalous search behavior," which explained why his staff inquired about her photo.[7]

OUTRAGE: THE CLEARVIEW CONTROVERSY

The publication of Hill's article in January 2020 ignited a firestorm of controversy. To identify suspects, police departments and government agencies in the United States had long searched databases of mugshots and driver licenses with facial recognition software. But, critics seethed, scraping billions of personal photographs and videos from the internet took privacy invasion to a whole new level. Ron Wyden, a Democratic Senator for Oregon, voiced this anger. "Americans have a right to know whether their personal photos are secretly being sucked into a private facial recognition database," he tweeted. "Every day we witness a growing need for strong federal laws to protect Americans' privacy."[8]

Privacy advocates, civil rights activists, and criminologists joined in the chorus of fury. The uproar grew even louder as news broke that employees in thousands of businesses, schools, and private security agencies across at least 27 countries – many without any formal permission from a superior – had used the Clearview app to run facial recognition searches, including those working for the NBA, Walmart, Best Buy, Home Depot, Macy's, Verizon, Bank of America, and Madison Square Garden. "Here's why it's concerning to me," said Clare Garvie, a privacy and technology researcher at Georgetown Law. "There is no clear line between who is permitted access to this incredibly powerful and incredibly risky tool and who doesn't have access. There is not a clear line between law enforcement and non-law enforcement."[9]

Activists, too, were upset to learn that campus police and school administrators across scores of universities had used the Clearview app. "This is exactly why we've been calling for administrators to enact a ban," said Evan Greer of Fight for the Future. "So much of this happens in secrecy. A security officer shouldn't be able to use this to stalk students around campus."[10]

Social media firms were angry, too. Facebook, Google, and Twitter issued cease-and-desist letters to Clearview AI, arguing the scraping of facial images violated their codes of conduct, privacy policies, and copyright laws. These firms further demanded that Clearview AI delete all biometric data collected from their platforms. Ton-That refused to comply, however, arguing his company had not violated any US laws, including anti-hacking laws. All he had ever done, he said, was scrape publicly available information from the internet. Ton-That shrugged when questioned about the ethics of scraping social media data. "A lot of people are doing it," he said. "Facebook knows."[11]

As publicity intensified, mayors and police chiefs across the world faced tough questions. Had any police officers relied on Clearview AI software? If so, did they have a warrant? If not, was anyone identified, arrested, or convicted based on information from Clearview AI?

New Jersey ordered its police departments to stop using the Clearview app, as did other jurisdictions. Many corporate executives also warned their security staff to avoid the technology. Facing multiple lawsuits, in May 2020 the company promised to cancel subscriptions for nongovernmental customers as well as suspend all sales in Illinois (where Clearview AI was facing a lawsuit for violating the state's 2008 Biometric Information Privacy Act).[12] This did not, however, appease civil liberties activists in the United States. "These promises do little to address concerns about Clearview's reckless and dangerous business model," said Nathan Freed Wessler, an ACLU attorney.[13]

Not surprisingly, this was not good for Clearview's business. Further setbacks, moreover, would soon follow. In June 2020, the European Data Protection Board warned police and intelligence agencies that facial recognition services like Clearview AI would "likely not be consistent with the EU data protection regime."[14] The following month, with Canadian privacy authorities investigating and Canadian lawsuits in the works, Clearview AI ended its services in Canada, including for the RCMP's National Child Exploitation Crime Centre (reportedly the company's last remaining Canadian client).[15] That month, too, privacy regulators in Australia and the UK launched a joint investigation into Clearview AI's data scraping and data management.[16] Clearview AI has also faced large fines for violating privacy and data collection laws, such as a €20 million fine by Italy's privacy agency in 2022.[17]

Yet the company has not gone bankrupt. Far from it. Clearview AI has managed to raise significant capital and sell its facial recognition services to police forces and intelligence agencies, claiming its software has helped "solve thousands of serious crimes," including sexual exploitation of children, sexual assault, and murder.[18] In August 2020, for instance, US Immigration and Customs Enforcement – known as ICE – signed a US$224,000 contract with the company.[19] Indeed, Ton-That says his company is prospering, with over 10 billion facial images now in its database, and with more than 3,100 law enforcement agencies having used its software in the US alone, including the FBI and the Department of Homeland Security.[20] The goal, the company is now saying, is to raise more capital, service private companies, and build out its database to 100 billion facial images so that "almost everyone in the world will be identifiable."[21]

Indicative of its ongoing use, there was a spike in Clearview AI searches after the January 6, 2021 attack on the US Capitol, as investigators across the United States (such as police officers in Alabama and Miami) used the software to identify rioters in video footage and social media photos (relaying this information to the FBI's Joint Terrorism Task Force, which had asked the public and local authorities for assistance in finding suspects).[22]

Another example of its ongoing use is in Ukraine, where, following the Russian invasion in February 2022, Ukrainian authorities began using the software (free of charge, according to Ton-That) to verify identities during street interrogations and at military checkpoints. In addition, the military and police have used the software to identify Russian soldiers, including those caught on video footage looting stores and homes, those captured by Ukrainian forces, and those killed in action – with Ukraine's volunteer "IT Army" then notifying families of the death of their child to try to spur opposition to the war within Russia.[23]

Ton-That, meanwhile, has been touting the value of his technology for tracing Covid-19 outbreaks. Asked by an NBC reporter if he was at all worried about the risks of enabling government authorities to track people for months on end, he replied: "It's really up to the agencies how they put these programs together. All we do is provide the identification part of the process."[24]

The story of Clearview AI reveals one of the toughest challenges for preventing the globalization – and gradual normalization – of facial recognition technology. Lawmakers will certainly ban some police departments from using the Clearview app, as happened in San Francisco and Boston. Regulations will undoubtedly restrain the company in places, as the EU's General Data Protection Regulation has done in Europe. Lawsuits and regulatory investigations will surely set the company back in some jurisdictions, as has happened in North America. One day soon the company could well go bankrupt. But this might not matter that much. There is a long line of tech entrepreneurs and stealth startups ready to take the place of Hoan Ton-That. There are, moreover, many other well-established tech firms willing to sell facial recognition products to police, security forces, schools, and private businesses.

THE FACIAL RECOGNITION INDUSTRY

As mentioned earlier, in June 2020 IBM mothballed its general-purpose facial recognition business. Shortly afterward, Amazon imposed a one-year moratorium on American police departments using its Rekognition service, while Microsoft pledged to only start selling facial recognition technology to these departments once the US Congress put in place a regulatory framework. The following year, Amazon extended its moratorium until further notice, while Meta, following a US$650 million class-action settlement and facing government inquiries and mounting criticism, announced it was "shutting down" Facebook's facial recognition system and deleting all facial recognition templates.[25] Retailers such as Home Depot, Kroger, Starbucks, Target, and Walmart have also pledged to not deploy the technology in their stores. The online world has trumpeted these decisions as victories for opponents of face surveillance technology. Yet many other multinational technology companies are still going full throttle to serve the facial recognition market, including for policing and surveillance.

NEC Corporation is a leader here. The company first began developing facial authentication software at the end of the 1980s. Today, its technology is one of the world's fastest, with an error rate as low as 0.5 percent on some US National Institute of Standards and Technology tests.[26] NEC's software is one of the best, too, in identifying people wearing facemasks, with the company reporting an accuracy rate of 99.9 percent in these cases.[27] Globally, NEC is a major exporter of facial authentication and surveillance technology, supplying a wide range of countries, from Argentina to Australia to India to Singapore to the United Kingdom (for instance, providing the Metropolitan Police serving Greater London with live facial recognition technology).[28]

Panasonic Corporation, which began developing facial recognition software in the early 1990s, is another market leader, integrating facial recognition capacity into an assortment of consumer and security products, including surveillance cameras. Toshiba is also a major player, operating more than 1,000 facial recognition projects in 2020, such as identity verification for border crossing and police checkpoints.[29] The Thales Group from France is at the forefront of this market too, offering a wide range of authentication and identification products for policing, passport control, voting, commercial transactions, background checks, and employee monitoring.[30]

Besides well-known transnational corporations, a large number of software companies are competing in this market, too. In 2020, at least 45 firms were selling live facial recognition technology, while at least 80 companies were offering face identification and verification products.[31] (With many startups working in the shadows, though, these figures could well be far higher.) Leading American biometrics firms, such as Aware and Animetrics, are competing in this market. So are Germany's Cognitec and Japan's Ayonix, which specialize in facial recognition software, including for surveillance and policing. And so is Australia's iOmniscient, which has sold facial recognition products across scores of countries, including to police departments in the United States.[32]

Asked if he intended to follow in the footsteps of Amazon and halt sales of facial recognition technology to US police departments, the CEO of iOmniscient, Rustom Kanga, replied: "I don't think taking technology away from [the police] is going to solve the problem." Sadi Vural, the CEO of Ayonix had a similar reaction. Police are "good customers," he said, and "there's no reason not to provide facial recognition technology to them."[33]

Competing in this market, too, are facial recognition startups with a speciality in artificial neural networks and deep learning techniques, such as Russia's NtechLab, which launched in 2016. The company sells a product called FindFace Security, which is able to identify faces in live video streams. Powered by machine learning, its facial recognition algorithm, the company claims, is both accurate and lightning fast, able to run an image through a dataset of one billion facial images in less than half a second. Its algorithm is especially adept at identifying faces in a crowd, according to NtechLab.

NtechLab markets FindFace Security to both corporations and state agencies, and says, unlike other facial recognition systems, that FindFace Security supports "an infinite number of video streams and facial database entries, ensuring the system offers unlimited scalability." NtechLab, moreover, is continuing to release new software every year, including an emotion recognition algorithm, which the company claims can identify "7 primary emotions and 50 compound emotions" to allow retailers and entertainment firms to measure customer satisfaction, moods, and desires.[34]

NtechLab has been thriving since its launch. To watch for soccer hooligans and pick-pockets during the 2018 FIFA World Cup, Russian authorities connected street, subway, and arena cameras to NtechLab's centralized facial recognition system.[35] Moscow has also integrated

FindFace technology into its closed-circuit television (CCTV) surveillance system, with a mobile app alerting officers when a wanted person is identified – enabling, according to the mayor of Moscow, Sergei Sobyanin, live facial recognition "on a mass scale."[36] Russian retailers, too, have installed NtechLab technology to identify repeat shoplifters as well as evaluate the age, gender, and reactions of customers to help optimize store displays and personalize service. At the same time, the company, with more than 100 corporate partnerships across 20 countries, is now working to sell its products to security forces and private businesses across Asia, Africa, and Latin America.[37]

All around the world companies like NtechLab are now starting up. Chinese firms are by far, however, the strongest force driving the surging market for face surveillance technology.

EXPORTING FACE SURVEILLANCE: THE ROLE OF CHINA

Chinese firms account for roughly half of the global market for facial recognition technology.[38] Relatively weak domestic privacy protections give Chinese firms an advantage over ones from North America and Europe, placing fewer constraints on data collection and commercial applications for policing and surveillance. By 2020, more than 50 countries had purchased components for facial recognition systems from Chinese companies, with at least 39 countries having bought facial recognition technology from Huawei alone.[39] Chinese firms are also core to the growing market for surveillance cameras, with Hikvision and Dahua accounting for around 40 percent of the global share in recent years.

Chinese startups such as SenseTime, Megvii, and CloudWalk are playing a leading role in this market, too. CloudWalk, for instance, is developing a facial image database and integrating facial recognition software into a national surveillance system in Zimbabwe. SenseTime's facial recognition technology has been integrated into the surveillance system of a high-security prison in Inner Mongolia. And, as Huawei installs high-speed wireless, Megvii is supplying facial recognition software to the government of Thailand.

The Chinese state is backing the export of facial recognition technology and cameras, especially to other authoritarian states looking to enhance domestic surveillance systems. Chinese banks and development agencies are providing financing and soft loans. Chinese engineers are training operational staff. Chinese officials are providing policy advice, helping local authorities pitch face surveillance as a way to advance "public security," "good governance," "smart cities," and "safe cities."[40] And, more broadly, Chinese corporate executives and officials are lobbying the United Nations International Telecommunication Union to shape the standards for video surveillance systems and facial recognition technology.[41] China's strategic plan to lead the world in artificial intelligence by 2030 is partly spurring this financing, technical assistance, and lobbying. But state support for the export of face surveillance technology would also seem to be part of a broader effort by China to challenge – and change – political and legal understandings of privacy and human rights.[42]

China's central role in the face surveillance industry creates significant challenges for local activists in developing countries. In Ecuador, for instance, activists have been able to reach out to civil society groups within Europe and North America to impede sales of high-tech surveillance equipment from companies headquartered in these places. Yet they have been unable to form advocacy networks within China, and Chinese firms such as Huawei, facing no opposition from within China, have been quick to supply face surveillance technology to Ecuador.[43]

China is not just leading the charge to export facial recognition technology. It is also, as the next chapter documents, at the forefront of normalizing the use of the technology at home.

8. The everyday politics of facial recognition in China

For years, people – mostly, it would seem, frugal seniors and impoverished migrants – had been slipping into the lavatories in Beijing's Temple of Heaven park to stuff toilet paper into their backpacks and bags, for later use. To stop such thievery, park staff came up with an ingenious solution: have a machine, following a facial scan, dispense a two-foot sheet of toilet paper. If more was necessary, one would need to wait patiently, as the machine only bestowed toilet paper to the same face every nine minutes.

As a bonus, staff upgraded the toilet paper from one- to two-ply. Staff promised to be on hand, too, if a park visitor were to suffer a true crisis demanding reams of toilet paper. "If we encounter guests who have diarrhoea or any other situation in which they urgently require toilet paper, then our staff on the ground will directly provide the toilet paper," explained a spokesperson for the park.[1]

Not everyone was happy when the facial recognition toilet paper dispensers were trialed in 2017. "The sheets are too short," grumbled Wang Jianquan, a retiree in his sixties.[2] Park regulars who spoke with CNN, however, were supportive. "They should have done this decades ago," said Zhang Shaomin. "I think it's necessary" to stop people from "wasting public resources," added Wu Qingqi. Even issues of privacy and dignity did not seem to perturb Liu Mei, a homemaker who was visiting the park when CNN approached her. "People come here for free toilet paper, they have already lost their self dignity," she said. "Do you think they would understand what personal privacy is?"[3]

Impressed with the results, local authorities across China were soon installing facial recognition toilet paper dispensers in other public washrooms, with some offering each face as much as three feet of toilet paper every nine minutes.[4] And, with these dispensers reducing toilet paper usage by as much as 70 percent, even more would seem to be on the way.[5]

No other country has gone as far as China in normalizing facial recognition technology. Nor does any country, as we saw in Chapter 7, have such a powerful corporate–state alliance backing the technology. To get a better sense of China's reach in the global political economy of facial recognition, let's look further into how the Communist Party of China is deploying the technology to enhance state surveillance and policing.

SURVEILLANCE AND POLICING

There are now hundreds of millions of surveillance cameras in China, by far the most of any country. Indicative, 16 of the world's 20 most surveilled cities in 2021 were in China. Taiyuan in Shanxi province in North China was the world's most surveilled city, with 117 CCTV cameras in place for every 1,000 residents. Wuxi in Jiangsu province in eastern China was second, with 90 cameras per 1,000 residents. Nationally, analysts are projecting China's surveillance network will exceed half-a-billion CCTV cameras in 2022, accounting for around half of the world's CCTV cameras.[6]

Across China, tens of millions of these CCTV cameras already have facial recognition capacity, and the Communist Party of China is aiming for blanket coverage of the country. Authorities are installing facial recognition cameras on lampposts, entranceways, and buildings to track Muslim Uyghurs in the Xinjiang region, enforce isolation orders during epidemics, and watch who goes in and out of public housing.[7] National security forces, meanwhile, are using facial recognition software to monitor a watch list of 20 to 30 million people.[8]

China is also at the forefront of many other face surveillance technologies. Detectives are using facial recognition cameras to identify fugitives at concerts and locate missing persons in homeless shelters. Traffic authorities are deploying these cameras to identify a driver who runs a red light or a pedestrian who jaywalks. Health authorities are using facial recognition technology to scan crowds to identify people with a high temperature or not wearing a facemask during disease outbreaks (such as during the Covid-19 pandemic). And hundreds of airports are screening passengers with facial recognition technology.

To help comply with government regulations, meanwhile, social media platforms are using AI-powered facial recognition software to flag videos and photographs containing "sensitive people," such as those who appear to be Uyghurs.[9] Building managers, too, are working with local authorities to install facial recognition cameras in apartment elevators to watch for "suspicious" visitors. In Shanghai alone, at least a third of the city's 10,000 apartment complexes now have face surveillance cameras, with more on the way.[10]

Cities such as Beijing, too, have installed facial recognition cameras in low-income rental housing projects to prevent illegal subletting and, according to authorities, protect residents. Complaints about the deepening of state surveillance of ordinary people have been surfacing in online chats. Publicly, however, at least some residents in these housing projects are lending their support. "We feel much more secure now," one resident told Xinhua, the Chinese state news agency.[11] Even when not speaking with the state news agency, many residents across China would appear to agree, with one survey by the Nandu Personal Information Protection Research Center finding that 60–70 percent of people feel that facial recognition is making the country safer.[12] Another survey, by scholars from Europe, found only 9 percent of respondents in China somewhat or strongly opposed to facial recognition technology: a much lower number than in the United Kingdom (22 percent), the United States (25 percent), and Germany (31 percent).[13]

That said, many Chinese citizens have concerns. The Nandu Center's survey found that four-fifths of people think China's facial recognition systems do not adequately protect data, while more than half worry about the increasing use of facial recognition to track people's movements. Indicative of these concerns, three-quarters of those polled said they would like to retain the option of verifying transactions and identities with traditional forms of identification.[14]

Also revealing are the occasional criticisms of facial recognition technology on Chinese social media, with comments on sites such as Weibo (similar to Twitter) like: "Big brother is keeping an eye on you – George Orwell's 1984." A few Chinese human rights activists have been openly critical too, such as Ou Biaofeng of Hunan province, who told a reporter: "This type of technology is mainly used by the dictators to tighten social controls. With it, they can easily find those who criticize the government or dissidents who hold different political views."[15]

Some activists have also challenged the value of intensifying face surveillance to control the Covid-19 pandemic. "When we go out or stay in a hotel, we can feel a pair of eyes looking at us at any time," activist Wang Aizhong (who lives in Guangzhou) was already telling the *Guardian* in March of 2020. "We are completely exposed to the monitoring of the government." The long-term worry for one resident of the city of Chengdu is obvious: "Because this method has been used before, citizens will accept it. It becomes normal."[16]

There is, however, very little organized resistance to face surveillance in China – and nothing close to the civil society pushback seen in Europe and North America. Chinese activists and social media influencers are not a major force within the transnational social movement contesting facial recognition technology. Nor, in any visible way, are transnational networks of privacy and rights activists hindering the uptake in China of facial recognition technology. This is hardly surprising given China's offline and online suppression of civil society organizations advocating for civil liberties, human rights, or political reforms.[17]

For the most part, moreover, policing applications of facial recognition in China have been garnering favorable publicity in the Chinese press. One example is Baidu's AI-powered facial recognition searching technology. China's Ministry of Civil Affairs, along with local rescue centers, have been using Baidu's technology to locate missing children, in some cases by matching a decades-old photograph of a child with a recent picture of them as an adult. This technology, according to Baidu, has helped reunite thousands of missing children with their families.[18]

FACIAL RECOGNITION TECHNOLOGY IN SCHOOLS

Schools across China, meanwhile, are starting to install face surveillance and analysis systems. Schools are especially powerful normalizing forces for new technology, able to mold new generations who will know of no other reality. Seeing hundreds of children in cities such as Shenzhen quickly scan their faces to rush through the entrance gates of their elementary school brings this home.[19] The integration of FRT into schools in China, moreover, looks set to pick up speed over the next decade, as parents and administrators embrace the technology as a way to enhance student safety, prevent bullying, and improve the quality of teaching.

Social media posts do voice concerns over the risks of data breaches and privacy infringements of minors. Online postings have also questioned the value of using algorithmic analysis of facial expressions to cajole students into learning. "Why not get students' attention through improving lesson quality," wondered one Weibo user.[20] Now and then, commentaries in local newspapers and state media have urged caution, too.[21] A few educators have also spoken out against the technology, such as Peking University's Cao Qingjiu, who worries about the psychological effects on adolescents. "They need respect and trust from others," he said. "Installing such a system may trigger students' antipathy against it to the extreme."[22]

Still, with increasing numbers of Chinese facial recognition firms competing hard to expand educational markets, and with the Chinese Communist Party backing a deepening of AI surveillance, the technology is now making its way into elementary schools, high schools, and universities. Some schools are monitoring entrance gates and dormitories with the technology, replacing traditional identification cards. Some are setting up cashless cafeterias. Some are using it to take attendance. Some are tracking the comings and goings of students to watch out for tardiness and bullying. Some are monitoring the health and movements of students to prevent disease outbreaks. And some are evaluating the facial expressions of students to judge levels of boredom, skepticism, and distraction.[23]

One example is the China Pharmaceutical University in Nanjing, which began piloting facial analysis technology in 2019. The technology takes attendance and notes if a student leaves class early. It tracks, too, whether students listen attentively to lectures, raise their hands with interest, look sleepy, or become distracted by their smartphones. The system, explains university administrator Xu Jianzhen, is "targeted at improving the students' attendance rate and enhancing the classroom discipline." Asked if it might infringe on privacy rights, as some were saying on social media, he was dismissive: "there is no such thing as 'infringement of privacy' since the classroom is a public place."[24]

Another example is the elementary school affiliated with Shanghai University of Traditional Medicine, which is using an AI-powered facial recognition system to track when students smile, if they greet their teacher properly, and whether they pick up litter without being asked. It also watches the teacher and recommends ways to improve performance: what is described as "the intelligent teacher training system."[25]

Uptake of facial recognition technology across China's schools surged in 2020 as administrators looked for ways to contain the Covid-19 pandemic. Peking University in Beijing, which was already relying on facial recognition gates for entry, installed cameras throughout the campus to ensure fast and accurate facial recognition contact tracing if a student fell ill. "All of a sudden we found dozens of cameras in our dorm building, six on each floor," said one student. "It's like someone is watching you from when you wake up to when you go to sleep," said another. Asked if students were worried the surveillance would remain in place after the pandemic ended, she shrugged: "I think there is that concern among students, but there's no option but to accept it."[26]

A FACE-SCAN ECONOMY

Across China, facial scanning to verify identities and authenticate transactions is another powerful force normalizing facial recognition technology. China is already well on its way to becoming a cashless society as people pay for goods and services with online payment services such as WeChat Pay and Alipay. Since the end of 2019 anyone purchasing a SIM card in China has had to submit to a facial scan, ostensibly to prevent identity fraud and enhance the security of the cashless economy. Some retailers, meanwhile, are going further, allowing customers to pay directly with facial scanning. After ordering or selecting a product, a customer simply looks into the camera and gives a thumbs up to authorize the purchase.

Residents in China are also scanning their faces to deliver packages without needing to show identification, provide payment details, or fill out a home address. They are scanning their faces to withdraw money and pay taxes. They are scanning their faces to pay for subway rides, replacing slower scanning of tickets or phones. They are scanning their faces to walk into gyms and amusement parks. And they are scanning their faces to gain access to online gaming sites, as companies such as Tencent turn to FRT to try to enforce laws that limit the playing time of adolescents.[27]

Unlike with surveillance, security, and policing, there has been little criticism in China of the growing reach of facial recognition technology into the cashless economy. Indeed, according to Professor Ouyang Liangyi at Peking University's HSBC Business School, facial payment is proving to be "quite popular" among Chinese consumers, as it is easy, convenient, and fast, allowing payment even without a smartphone.[28]

Not everyone, however, is ready to sacrifice privacy for convenience. Professor Guo Bing of Zhejiang Sci-Tech University in eastern China, for instance, sued the Hangzhou Safari Park in 2019 for requiring face identification for entry, claiming this breaches consumer protection law.[29] The court ruled in Guo's favor, directing the Zoo to delete his facial scans and compensate him with about 1,000 yuan. The court refused, though, to rule on the legality of requiring face identification, treating the case as a contractual dispute and allowing the Zoo to continue to require a facial scan for entry. Guo appealed, but the court upheld its original ruling in late 2020, only additionally directing the Zoo to delete

Guo's fingerprints. Referencing Guo's case, however, in 2021 China's Supreme People's Court did set new regulatory guidelines requiring businesses to seek customer consent, enhance data protections, and only use facial recognition technology when "necessary."[30]

Others in China, too, are challenging the use of facial recognition technology. One example is Lao Dongyan, a law professor at Tsinghua University in Beijing, who managed to stop her residential compound from requiring facial recognition for entry, and instead making it optional (residents can also gain access with an identification card or mobile phone).[31]

Still, despite grumblings here and there, and despite some wins for privacy and consumer rights advocates, China is well on its way to normalizing facial recognition technology, making it a largely unquestioned, even expected and demanded, part of politics, the economy, and everyday life. Other countries, too, are following in China's footsteps, with, as the next chapter discusses, many picking up their pace in recent years.

9. The globalization of facial recognition technology

Governments far beyond China are now installing facial recognition cameras on streetlights, at traffic intersections, and atop buildings. Police officers are wearing live facial recognition body cameras. Detectives are identifying suspects with facial recognition software. Health authorities are enforcing stay-at-home orders with facial recognition cameras. And guards are monitoring the comings and goings of prisoners with facial security systems.

Researchers at Pennsylvania's Harrisburg University of Science and Technology have even worked on developing facial analysis software to predict whether a person will one day commit a criminal act. "With 80 percent accuracy and with no racial bias," claimed a 2020 press release by Harrisburg University, "the software can predict if someone is a criminal based solely on a picture of their face."[1] Analysts and activists all around the world dismissed the press release as snake oil marketing. "It's just stupid to think that a photograph or any biometric can predict future actions," reacted law professor Andrew Guthrie Ferguson.[2] Still, Jonathan W. Korn, one of the researchers and a former New York police officer, sees high future demand for such software. "Identifying the criminality of a person from their facial image," he said, "will enable a significant advantage for law enforcement agencies and other intelligence agencies to prevent crime from occurring in their designated areas."[3]

Global demand for FRT systems is also rising for healthcare, education, and banking. Nurses are using facial recognition technology to confirm patient identities and drug dosages. School security staff are deploying the technology to watch for known drug dealers and registered sex offenders. Banks are offering face recognition as an option for authenticating online transactions requiring multiple identifications. And customers are paying with face recognition to avoid touching screens or exchanging money with a cashier.

There are, moreover, thousands of other possible examples of the spread of facial recognition technology. Retailers are deploying the technology to estimate the age, gender, and backgrounds of consumers to better target advertising. Manufacturers are relying on facial recognition cameras to clock workers in and out of factories. Sports stadiums are screening fans with FRT to keep out barred hooligans, eliminate long lineups, and, in the words of Panasonic's Gerard Figols, "offer peace of mind to fans."[4] Meanwhile, every day, hundreds of millions of people are using face recognition to unlock their smartphones, tablets, and computers.

In part, the global market for facial recognition products is expanding because the technology is improving. The recognition algorithms are gaining proficiency, able to better account for aging, poor lighting, bad angles, and masked faces. And the databanks of faces are expanding as security cameras proliferate, people submit to facial scans, programmers scrape facial images from social media, "free" apps surreptitiously collect photographs and videos for training facial recognition algorithms, and officials upload mugshots, driver licenses, and passport photos. Testing confirms the increasing proficiency of facial recognition software, with the US National Institute of Standards and Technology finding "massive gains in accuracy" since 2013.[5]

Demand for particular applications of FRT, however, varies widely. So, too, does the speed and nature of the normalization of the technology in different countries of the world.

CHARGING FORWARD IN THE ASIA-PACIFIC

Uptake of facial recognition technology is rising quickly across the Asia-Pacific. China, as Chapter 8 documented, is well out in front. Yet usage is rising in many other countries in the Asia-Pacific, too, from passengers at Tokyo's Narita International Airport speeding up boarding to hotel guests in Singapore fast-tracking check-in.

Japanese companies are leaders in the global facial recognition market. At home, Japan is steadily integrating the technology into banking, cashless payment systems, airport security, school administration, government services, stadium security, and the monitoring of Covid-19. Japan is also increasingly relying on the technology for police work. Detectives are using it, for instance, to match the photos of suspects with images on social media and in surveillance footage. "We are using the system only for criminal investigations and within the scope of law," said one police official when justifying the practice.[6]

Singapore is also moving quickly toward normalizing facial recognition technology. The Singaporean government has integrated facial verification into immigration controls, government apps, and the national identity scheme. It is working to install more than 100,000 facial recognition cameras across the country. And it is rolling out face identification kiosks to access state services (relying on its national biometric database to verify identities). Given such trends, Steven Wong, the president of Singapore's Association of Information Security Professionals, sees little choice but to accept the technology as part of daily life. "As facial recognition becomes increasingly adopted, both overseas and locally, it is inevitable that people will just have to be accustomed to it," he said.[7]

Malaysia, too, is integrating facial recognition into policing, surveillance networks, and everyday life. The technology is verifying identities and tracking passengers at Kuala Lumpur International Airport. Police are using it to identify faces caught on bodycams. And state governments are integrating it into CCTV surveillance systems. Penang's Chief Minister Chow Kon Yeow was exuberant when launching a facial recognition surveillance system for his state. "Wanted persons can be traced using this system," he said, "and this system is fully linked with the police operations room in Penang."[8]

At the same time, increasing numbers of Malaysian citizens are relying on facial recognition to pay for goods, authenticate transactions, and enter event venues. Anitha Krishnan, who works for a software company specializing in event planning, sees a bright future in Malaysia for facial recognition check-in. "There will be an increase every year," she predicted in 2019, after noting a rise in demand over the previous two years. "People are not going backwards and always wanting to try something new."[9]

In India, meanwhile, the government of Prime Minister Narendra Modi is aiming for facial identification of all 1.4 billion residents. Already, the technology is being widely used for policing, identity verification, and surveillance, with at least 16 different governmental FRT systems already in place across the country by 2021.[10] For instance, Delhi police, which first began using facial recognition software in 2018 to identify street children, deployed the technology to remove "habitual protesters" and "rowdy elements" from a 2019 political rally for Prime Minister Modi.[11]

Police in Delhi and the northern state of Uttar Pradesh have also used facial recognition software to identify those protesting against a 2019 amendment to India's Citizenship Act. (This amendment infuriated many Muslims across India, as it made non-Muslim minorities who fled persecution in Afghanistan, Bangladesh, and Pakistan eligible for citizenship: what some describe as the "anti-Muslim" law.) The software, for instance, identified more than 1,000 people involved in two days of rioting in Delhi in February 2020. India's Home Minister, Amit Shah, was dismissive when asked whether facial recognition software should be used for such purposes given the possibility of false positives. "This is a software," he said. "It does not see faith. It does not see clothes. It only sees the face and through the face the person is caught."[12]

Facial recognition technology is spreading across Australia, too, even in the face of pushback from domestic civil liberties, privacy, and human right organizations.[13] The federal government is creating a national database of mugshots, passport pictures, and license photos to enable intelligence, policing, and civil agencies to verify identities with facial recognition software.[14] Schools are monitoring premises with facial recognition cameras, sending alerts to staff if an unknown face enters, an unauthorized person tries to pick up a child, or a student is missing from class. Senior citizen homes and daycares are installing facial recognition kiosks to monitor premises, while businesses are using the technology to clock employees in and out of work. As elsewhere, the Covid-19 pandemic sparked further interest in the technology, with, for instance, the Australian firm, LoopLearn, marketing its facial recognition kiosks as "hands free" – a "fast, hygienic, and easy" way to sign in and out of schools, retirement homes, and workplaces.[15]

RISING UPTAKE IN NORTH AMERICA

Civil society resistance to facial recognition technology, as we saw in Part II of this book, is especially strong in the United States. In Canada, too, an activist coalition has formed to lobby for a national ban on the use of the technology for policing and mass surveillance. At the same time, however, a myriad of North American companies and startups are marketing new applications of the technology, with national regulations doing little to constrain them.

In this context, uptake of FRT is rising across North America, although with less demand for street surveillance and policing applications than in the Asia-Pacific. The North American market is steadily expanding, however, for applications that verify identities, authenticate financial transactions, enhance security, and automate healthcare and hospitality services. There are signs, too, of growing societal acceptance of FRT – or at least acquiescence – for accessing consumer devices, validating IDs, and passing through security checkpoints.

Consider the Maynard H. Jackson International Terminal at the Hartsfield–Jackson Atlanta International Airport, the first biometric terminal in the United States. In partnership with US Customs and Border Protection and the US Transport Security Administration, Delta Air Lines integrated FRT into this terminal to authorize check-in, verify passenger identities, and speed up boarding. Passengers can easily opt out. But less than 2 percent are doing so. According to polls commissioned by Delta Air Lines, more than 90 percent of passengers have "no issue" using facial recognition for boarding, while more than 70 percent prefer it.[16]

Scores of other US airports have also integrated FRT into check-in, boarding, and security checks. To identify visa overstayers, for instance, since 2017 US Customs and Border Protection has been using facial recognition software to screen passengers who are leaving the United States: a "biometric exit" that Homeland Security says is on track to cover more than 97 percent of international departures by 2023.[17] Airports across the US are also now screening arriving passengers with facial recognition software, with three in 2019, 14 in 2020, and 182 in 2021 installing this technology. Facial recognition systems now screen 99 percent of passengers on flights entering the United States, according to US Customs and Border Protection.[18] Airports in Canada are also deploying facial recognition technology, such as in the NEXUS kiosks at the Vancouver International Airport, the Toronto Pearson International Airport, the Montréal–Pierre Elliott Trudeau International Airport, and the Halifax Stanfield International Airport.

Airports in North America have a history of normalizing new security technologies, from metal detectors to X-ray machines to full-body scanners. This looks set to occur for facial recognition technology, too. "The same way that travelers automatically know to lift their arms and spread their feet for airport security's full-body scanners today," notes tech analyst Dave Gershgorn, "lifting your chin so the camera can take a better picture of your face at a CBP [Customs and Border Protection] checkpoint or facial recognition check-in will become rote." With facial recognition becoming the new "gold standard" for airport security, he argues, it will not take long before schools, government buildings, amusement parks, and sports stadiums also consider it best practice.[19]

This is already starting to occur. Manhattan's Madison Square Garden has integrated facial recognition into its security systems. Basketball's Dallas Mavericks is using facial recognition to prevent unauthorized visitors from entering its locker room and training facilities. Baseball's New York Mets and soccer's Los Angeles Football Club are experimenting with facial recognition gates to enable quick and "touchless" entry for players, staff, and season-ticket holders who choose to opt in.[20] Residential and commercial buildings in many cities are installing facial recognition cameras to enhance security. So are schools across the United States, with parental support strong in many districts, especially following mass shootings.[21]

One example is the Texas City Independent School District. A 45-minute drive southeast of Houston, this public district comprises around 8,600 students across seven elementary schools, three middle schools, and four high schools.[22] Three days after a 2017 mass shooting at a high school in the neighboring city of Santa Fe, the Texas City Independent School District hired Mike Matranga as executive director of security and school safety. Matranga has unusual credentials for school staff, having previously been a counter-assault Secret Service agent and a member of Barack Obama's protection detail. "I knew we needed to do something different," remarked the district superintendent, Rodney Cavness. "I hired an expert and let him do the job."[23]

Matranga went straight to work, staffing his unit with military veterans, coating school windows in bullet-resistant film, reinforcing classroom doors, and mounting security cameras. He bought software to monitor social media for signs of threats and set up an app to allow students and parents to submit anonymous tips. For good measure, at each school he installed gun safes with lightweight, AR-15 semi-automatic rifles. "You meet superior firepower with superior firepower," he reasoned. Besides, as he said in a later interview, "it just makes the fight fair."[24]

On top of this, Matranga's security team installed facial recognition technology to scan live video feeds for people on a school watch list. This list includes expelled students, registered sex offenders, known drug dealers, and individuals who, in Matranga's words, are "irrational" and "unstable," such as one woman who called him an "asshole" during a heated argument at a school board meeting (he uploaded her Facebook profile picture to the school watch list). When the facial security system spots someone on this watch list, a siren wails and an alert is sent to Matranga's team as well as to local deputy sheriffs.[25]

Matranga does not apologize for intensifying school surveillance: "You have surveillance cameras at Disney World, why should schools be different?" Nor does he have much time for critics who say his security measures violate privacy rights, infringe upon civil liberties, cause psychological harm, or risk aggravating racial inequality. "People need to stop being so sensitive," he said. "Facts and data are facts and data. I don't make them up. We take it and build from it and we identify kids at risk."[26]

Texas City Independent School District is just one of many school districts in North America installing facial recognition technology. To authorize and log entry into buildings and rooms, for instance, dozens of US schools are deploying a RealNetworks system known as "SAFR" (pronounced "safer," and standing for secure, accurate facial recognition). Rob Glaser, the CEO of RealNetworks and a former Microsoft executive, is expecting even greater uptake in the near future, with districts comprising more than a thousand schools having "expressed interest" in using SAFR.[27] Founded by Glaser in 1994, RealNetworks is a Seattle-based software company best known for advancing audio and video streaming over the internet (through products such as RealPlayer). The company began developing SAFR in 2015, training it using millions of facial images from RealTimes, a free app that automatically creates photo slideshows and video stories. (This was legal under the terms of RealTimes' 3,300-word user agreement.)

By 2018, SAFR was precise enough to tell identical twins apart, and adept at recognizing faces in candid, unposed, poorly lit, and oddly angled photographs and video frames. It was also capable of real-time recognition of faces in live video feeds from Internet Protocol (IP) cameras, while requiring less bandwidth and computing power than many competing facial recognition products. Company tests, meanwhile, were attaining a 99.86 percent recognition accuracy rate after just one-tenth of a second of processing time.

RealNetworks is marketing SAFR as offering 24/7 security for businesses, casinos, museums, hospitals, stadiums, airports, schools, military complexes, and government offices anywhere in the world. "SAFR for Security is powerful because it works – it's fast, accurate, and reliable in a surprising number of adverse conditions," says Dae-Jun Lee, a manager at South Korea's SK Telecom.[28] SAFR also has the capacity to gauge the age, gender, and emotional state of those caught on camera. "SAFR for Security," explains a staff member at the Carroll Shelby race car museum in Las Vegas, "helps us understand who is moving through our museum by age, gender, and time of day – allowing us to better tailor our museum experience."[29]

Besides selling SAFR, the company is offering the software for free to K-12 schools in Canada and the United States, as a way, according to

CEO Rob Glaser, to give back to the community by increasing school safety. "We are proud to give our SAFR for K-12 technology solution to every elementary, middle and high school in America and Canada," he said. "We hope this will help make schools safer."[30]

Not everyone is grateful. Critics are portraying SAFR as an invasion of privacy with little, if any, value for enhancing school safety. There is a real risk too, critics add, of aggravating discriminatory schooling. "The use of facial recognition in schools creates an unprecedented level of surveillance and scrutiny," argues John Cusick, a litigator at the NAACP Legal Defense and Educational Fund. "It can exacerbate racial disparities in terms of how schools are enforcing disciplinary codes and monitoring their students."[31]

But many commentators are defending the technology, too. "There's no panacea here," said Oren Etzioni, the CEO of Seattle's Allen Institute for Artificial Intelligence. "But I do think that trading some degree of privacy is a reasonable trade-off for saving children's lives."[32]

GOING GLOBAL: FROM EUROPE TO AFRICA TO LATIN AMERICA

Sales of facial recognition technology are also rising in Europe, although, like in North America, demand for street surveillance and policing applications is weaker than in the Asia-Pacific, as privacy and civil rights groups push back and governments begin to impose regulatory measures. The United Kingdom, however, is beginning to integrate facial recognition into its network of surveillance cameras. The Metropolitan Police of Greater London, for instance, has deployed live facial recognition cameras to search for suspects on government watch lists, although this has generated a storm of protests and legal challenges from privacy and civil liberty organizations.[33] Museums, shopping malls, casinos, and real estate developers are also using the technology to enhance traditional security systems. Supermarkets, meanwhile, are using facial recognition cameras to estimate the age of customers purchasing tobacco or alcohol. Looking around the UK, the privacy advocacy organization Big Brother Watch argues the technology is spreading like an "epidemic" through the country's private businesses.[34]

Businesses in other European countries are deploying the technology, too. The Brøndby IF football club in the Danish Superliga, for instance, began using Panasonic's FacePRO at Brøndby Stadium in 2019: the first club to do so in Denmark. Airport authorities across the European

Union, meanwhile, are using facial recognition to automate passport controls, enabling citizens to bypass long customs lines. Governments are investing as well in facial recognition for policing and surveillance. By 2020, police in at least 11 countries in the European Union were using facial recognition technology, with police in at least another eight EU countries planning to do so in the near future.[35] In the Hungarian capital of Budapest, for instance, there are now tens of thousands of surveillance cameras with facial recognition capacity.

Cities across Russia are also integrating facial recognition into CCTV surveillance cameras, as Moscow did a few years back. Russia's corporate world, as the story of NtechLab's in Chapter 7 illustrates, is embracing the technology too. One revealing example is the search engine Yandex, which, after a 2019 upgrade, was allowing users to search a facial image for matches and linked websites, enabling anyone – from a stalker to a blackmailer to an intelligence officer – to snap a photo, run it through Yandex, and potentially identify a person in a matter of seconds. Felix Rosbach, who works for a German software company, described Yandex's image search as "creepy," but added: "This isn't just poor from Yandex, this is (unfortunately) the future that we live in."[36]

Facial recognition markets are growing as well in Africa and Latin America, although more slowly than in Asia, Europe, and North America. Technology firms headquartered in Japan, Europe, and North America are all striving to make inroads into these markets. Chinese companies, as Chapter 7 documents, are also exporting facial recognition surveillance and policing technologies across the developing world. China's geopolitical strategy to build bilateral bridges with other authoritarian states is another powerful force diffusing FRT into Africa and Latin America. Kenya, South Africa, Uganda, and Zimbabwe, for example, have all integrated Chinese-made facial recognition into surveillance systems. So, too, have countries such as Bolivia, Brazil, Ecuador, and Venezuela.[37]

In Uganda, for instance, the administration of President Yoweri Museveni has integrated Huawei facial recognition technology into a nationwide network of CCTV surveillance cameras. The technology is helping investigators solve violent crimes and track down fugitives. But it is also being used to catalogue the identities of people who attend the rallies of Museveni's opponents. And it is helping Ugandan police identify and round up anti-government demonstrators, including hundreds of people caught on CCTV footage protesting the arrest of two presidential candidates in November 2020.[38] "The CCTV project is just a tool to track us, hunt us and persecute us," said Ingrid Turinawe, chair of the Women's League of the Forum for Democratic Change (FDC), a Ugandan opposition party.[39] President Museveni, who has been in power since 1986, looks set to deepen high-tech surveillance even further during his record sixth term of office that began in 2021.

In Ecuador, meanwhile, the capital city of Quito has installed Chinese-made facial recognition technology for street-level surveillance, policing, and airport security. Similarly, La Paz, the capital city of Bolivia, has installed Chinese-made facial recognition cameras as part of a smart-city project. "The goal of these systems is to have control, even if people feel harassed and observed," argues Cesar Ortiz Anderson, who heads up the nongovernmental Peruvian Pro-Citizen Security Association. "The authorities can use these tools for repression, just like they do in China and other authoritarian countries."[40]

Dozens of cities across Brazil are also integrating facial recognition software into policing and surveillance technologies, with Chinese and American firms competing especially hard for a share of the growing Brazilian market. In recent years, for instance, city police have been scanning video and drone footage with facial recognition software to identify fugitives during the annual Carnival street parties, with hundreds arrested in 2019 and 2020.[41] Schools across Brazil are also installing facial recognition systems to take attendance, enhance school security, and alert parents in real time when students are absent.[42]

Argentina, too, is deploying live facial recognition surveillance technology, including in the subways of Buenos Aires to alert police when spotting a face in the national database of open arrest warrants for serious crimes. According to an investigation by Human Rights Watch, this online database contains "significant errors," and includes photos and personal information of children under the age of 18 who have committed minor offenses.[43] Activists have called on the city of Buenos Aires to suspend its facial recognition technology for identifying fugitives, arguing it is unreliable, error prone, and violates privacy and children's rights. The city's Justice and Security Ministry has pushed back, though, arguing the technology is an effective and legal policing tool.[44]

In the past, uptake of FRT in Africa and Latin America has been impeded by higher inaccuracy rates when identifying people from these regions. This would seem to be changing, however. International software firms are working to improve the technology. Startups from Africa and Latin America, too, are tackling this problem. To enable a business or bank to confirm a customer's identity remotely, for instance, Charlette N'Guessan and her team of Ghana-based software engineers devel-

oped more locally accurate facial verification by training the software
with black African faces – a feat that won the UK's Royal Academy
of Engineering 2020 Africa Prize for Engineering Innovation. "It is
essential to have technologies like facial recognition based on African
communities, and we are confident their innovative technology will have
far reaching benefits for the continent," said Rebecca Enonchong, one of
the prize judges.[45]

THE POLITICS AND ECONOMICS OF FACIAL RECOGNITION

The forces globalizing and normalizing facial recognition technology,
as this chapter shows, are diverse, diffuse, and extraordinarily powerful. Just about everywhere, corporations are integrating the technology
into consumer products and services. Governments are deploying it to
automate border controls, investigate crimes, and deepen surveillance.
Schools are installing it to enhance learning, teaching, and school safety.
And businesses are using it to analyze consumer reactions, enable
keyless entry for preferred customers, and watch for shoplifters. New and
improved facial recognition products, meanwhile, are cascading into the
global marketplace. Governing a technology that is advancing so quickly,
from so many different sources, and with so many different uses (both
good and bad) is exceptionally difficult for the global community.

The political power of the anti-FRT movement, as we saw in Part II, is
steadily rising, especially in Europe and North America. As this chapter
has revealed, however, at least so far civil society resistance has not been
able to stop the technology from becoming an increasingly normal part of
policing, surveillance, schools, airports, banking, business, and everyday
life, from paying online to crossing a border to entering a building.

Research by Comparitech, a consumer advocacy company supporting
online privacy and cybersecurity, supports this conclusion. Comparitech
analyzed the uptake of FRT across the world's 100 most populated
countries (excluding North Korea), focusing on the use by police, state
agencies, airports, banks, schools, public transit companies, and commercial businesses. Around 70 percent of the surveyed countries were
deploying the technology "on a large-scale basis," Comparitech found
in 2021. Banks and financial institutions were using the technology in
80 percent of the countries, police forces in 70 percent, airports in 60
percent, businesses in 40 percent, trains and subways in 30 percent,
and schools in 20 percent. More than 40 percent of the countries had

deployed the technology to try to contain the Covid-19 pandemic. Only a half-dozen countries (Burundi, Cuba, Haiti, Madagascar, South Sudan, and Syria) did not appear to be using the technology, not because of a ban or moratorium, however, but seemingly because of insufficient financing or infrastructure.[46]

China ranked first on Comparitech's list of countries with the most "widespread and invasive use" of facial recognition technology. Second was Russia, followed by the United Arab Emirates, Japan, India, Chile, Australia, Brazil, Argentina, France, Hungary, Malaysia, and the United Kingdom. Next, with equal scores, were Mexico and the United States.[47]

China, Uganda, and Myanmar ranked as the top three states deploying the technology in ways that disregard the privacy of citizens (what Comparitech describes as "invasive"). Belgium, meanwhile, was evaluated as having some of the world's strictest rules in place, only permitting the police, for instance, to use the technology with legal authorization and under exceptional circumstances. Very few countries, however, were found to have implemented stringent controls, and Comparitech's overall conclusion is telling: the worldwide uptake of facial recognition technology is increasing "at an exponential rate."[48]

This trajectory is not immutable, however, and, as this book has shown, the transnational social movement to resist facial recognition technology is growing in size, gaining strength, and pulling off notable victories. What does this suggest for the future of facial recognition technology?

PART IV

Conclusions

10. The future of facial recognition technology

The facial recognition market, we should keep in mind, would be growing even faster if not for the transnational social movement to rein in the use of facial recognition technology. Activists have slowed sales in Western Europe and North America. They have won court cases against firms deploying the technology in Asia, Latin America, and Eastern Europe. They have nudged transnational corporations such as Microsoft into more restrained development of the technology. They have pressured retailers into suspending sales of facial recognition products to police departments, as happened in 2020 with Amazon's Rekognition software for the US market. They have convinced firms to stop developing general-purpose facial recognition and analysis software, as IBM promised to do in 2020. And they have disrupted – and at times derailed – startups like Clearview AI that are quietly selling facial recognition services to law enforcement agencies.

As this book has documented, too, governments are starting to restrict the use of facial recognition technology, some with bans for policing and public services, as in San Francisco and Boston, others with regulatory guardrails, as in the US state of Washington. Portland's ordinance to forbid private businesses from using the technology in public spaces is an especially big win for activists in the United States. The influence of the anti-FRT movement is rising in Europe, too. Echoing civil society campaigns across Europe, in 2021 the governments of Germany, Belgium, and Slovakia, as well as the European Data Protection Board and the European Data Protection Supervisor, all expressed support for a Europe-wide ban on face surveillance of public spaces. That year, too, the European Parliament passed a resolution calling for a moratorium on the use of automated facial recognition for policing and state surveillance, while the UN High Commissioner for Human Rights called for a worldwide moratorium on the use of remote facial recognition in real time. Over this time, meanwhile, the European Commission was continuing to work on drafting legislation to limit the use of facial recognition technology within the European Union.

The influence of the anti-FRT movement has clearly been rising in recent years. Will this continue? If so, what are the prospects of one day containing the dangers of FRT? How might this vary across the world? What does the analysis of the consequences of the anti-FRT movement suggest more broadly for our understanding of the potential of transnational social movements to resist the globalization of new technologies? In this concluding chapter, I offer tentative – and admittedly speculative – answers to these questions.

EXTENDING THE POWER AND REACH OF ANTI-FRT ACTIVISM

The anti-FRT movement, as we have seen over the course of this book, is generating a groundswell of local resistance, particularly in places with strong civil societies and political cultures prioritizing rights, liberties, and democracy. A wide range of civil society organizations are now campaigning to rein in FRT, including Access Now, the Algorithmic Justice League, Amnesty International, the American Civil Liberties Union, Article 19, Big Brother Watch, the Electronic Frontier Foundation, the Electronic Privacy Information Center, European Digital Rights, Fight for the Future, Human Rights Watch, the Institute for Consumer Protection in Brazil, the Internet Freedom Foundation in India, Liberty, and the Public Voice coalition. Youth groups, community activists, artist-activists, scholar-activists, and social media influencers are further energizing the movement.

In the coming years, even more activists in even more places would seem set to join anti-FRT campaigns. This has the potential to extend the reach, depth, and diversity of resistance, bringing on board even more groups advocating for civil liberties, civil rights, digital rights, privacy rights, ethical AI, data privacy, human rights, LGBTQ+ rights, racial justice, Indigenous rights, labor rights, consumer rights, youth rights, environmental sustainability, freedom of expression, religious freedoms, corporate social responsibility (CSR), social justice, migrant rights, and the rights of marginalized communities.

Cooperation among those opposing FRT, meanwhile, looks likely to remain strong. The consistency of messaging may even increase as support for time-limited moratoriums wanes and calls for permanent bans grow louder. Activists are increasingly concluding that better algorithms, higher-quality databases, corporate codes of conduct, and regulatory guardrails will never suffice to prevent governments and businesses from abusing the technology. Societal support is rising quickly for outright bans for mass surveillance, routine policing, predictive policing (e.g., to watch for potential drug smugglers or suicide bombers), and facial analysis of police interrogations (e.g., to infer emotions or lies).[1] Support is growing, too, for bans on the use of technology by schools and businesses, including to enter buildings, track workers and students, prevent bullying and shoplifting, evaluate mental states and personality, and profile customers and passersby (e.g., classifying them by race, age, gender, sexual orientation, or political leanings).[2]

The power of the FRT movement looks set to continue to rise as the base grows, support diversifies, and messaging becomes clearer and louder. There is the possibility, too, of surges in strength. More campaigns calling for bans on the use of the technology in stores – such as the one Fight for the Future is coordinating – could extend the reach of the anti-FRT movement among groups advocating for consumer rights, CSR, and labor rights.[3] More campaigns calling for bans on automated recognition of gender and sexual orientation – such as the one Access Now is running in Europe – could extend the movement's reach among groups advocating for LGBTQ+ rights, social justice, and anti-discrimination laws.[4]

More participation by organizations advocating for labor rights, consumer rights, human rights, social justice, and CSR, especially local groups in the developing world, could further empower the movement and help diffuse the anti-FRT norm into places with weaker advocacy for civil liberties, civil rights, digital rights, and privacy rights. There is potential, too, for international human rights organizations such as Amnesty International and Human Rights Watch to intensify – and extend – current campaigns to ban the use of automated facial recognition for routine policing, mass surveillance, and discriminatory profiling.

Wider and deeper engagement by environmental organizations and activists could also significantly enhance the power and reach of the anti-FRT movement. Police and security agencies around the world, as we saw in Chapter 9, are increasingly deploying facial recognition technology to identify, track, and profile dissidents and street protestors. This represents a grave threat to local activists opposing logging, mining, plantations, dams, and development projects, especially in Asia, Africa, and Latin America, where, every year, hundreds of environmental activists and land defenders are murdered or go missing, with police, militaries, and corporations often complicit.[5]

Greenpeace USA is a participating organization in Fight for the Future's campaign to "Ban Facial Recognition" in the United States. Greenpeace USA is also independently backing calls by Black Lives Matter for Amazon to "permanently" end all sales of surveillance and facial recognition software to US police departments and federal agencies, including to US Immigration and Customs Enforcement for the tracking, detaining, and deporting of immigrants.[6]

So far, however, relatively few environmental organizations have campaigned for FRT controls, beyond signing open letters calling for bans or moratoriums.[7] This could well change in the near future, however, as the capacity of FRT to repress environmentalism comes to light.[8] A wide range of well-established international environmental organizations could end up participating actively in the anti-FRT movement, such as Friends of the Earth, Greenpeace International, Rainforest Action Network, Rainforest Alliance, Conservation International, 350.org, Earthjustice, the Environmental Law Defender Center, World Wildlife Fund/World Wide Fund for Nature (WWF), and Global Witness (which every year documents the murders of environmentalists). The backing of national and community environmental organizations across the developing world could further deepen the reach of anti-FRT activism, as could the voices of the activists and Indigenous peoples now risking their lives to stop ecological destruction.

UNEVEN INFLUENCE GOING FORWARD

Yet, as this book reveals too, great care is necessary to avoid overestimating the potential worldwide power of the transnational social movement to rein in facial recognition technology. Looking globally, at least in the near term, the movement looks likely to remain uneven and fragmented, comprising highly localized efforts interacting and overlapping with a weakly constituted transnational advocacy network.

Resistance is much stronger, as we have seen, within political cultures that prioritize liberty, privacy, and freedom, and with a history of civil rights activism. Geographically, the layers of resistance are thickest in North America and Europe, and thinnest in Asia, Africa, and Latin America. Opposition has been particularly strong in the United States. Even here, however, resistance varies widely across local political cultures, while state and federal controls over facial recognition technology lag badly behind municipalities such as San Francisco, Boston, and Portland. This explains why thousands of law enforcement agencies are continuing to use the technology across the United States. At the same time, resistance is especially weak in authoritarian regimes, including within China, which is leading the charge to deploy facial recognition policing tools and install face surveillance networks, doing so at home to control its citizens and doing so abroad to deepen geopolitical ties with other repressive states. The Covid-19 pandemic, moreover, briefly knocked the wind out of the movement across the world, and then opened up an opportunity for states and firms to accelerate the process of normalizing the technology by touting it as an effective way to enforce quarantines and protect citizens.

Taking a bird's-eye view, we can see that governments in much of the world are ignoring or suppressing critics, and increasing numbers of police departments and intelligence agencies are using the technology to investigate crimes and intensify surveillance. Airports and hotels are speeding up services with facial recognition software. Schools, shopping malls, and businesses are installing facial recognition cameras to enhance security. Startups are competing hard to develop new facial recognition technology. Transnational corporations are selling more facial recognition products in more places. And, as we have seen in this book, the technology is becoming a normal part of life for growing numbers of people – as a way to purchase goods, enter a sports stadium, and bypass lineups at border crossings.

What does this suggest for the future? The anti-FRT movement is not going away. Indeed, as I have argued, it looks likely to keep growing stronger. Seeing the bans on FRT across cities in the United States, seeing the mounting political support to ban remote biometric surveillance across the European Union, and seeing the anti-FRT norm spreading globally, it may even seem as if the movement could one day rid the world of the technology, at least for routine policing, mass surveillance, and discriminatory facial analysis.

The governments now deploying facial recognition technology to enhance societal controls, however, are exceptionally powerful. So are the firms profiting from the technology. And the resulting politics is cutthroat. Those backing the technology are infiltrating the corridors of power, building alliances, gutting regulation, and silencing critics. Even the firms lobbying to regulate the technology in the United States are aiming to expand – not contract – markets. "They are calling for regulation of facial recognition," explains Evan Greer of Fight for the Future, "because they know their lawyers and lobbyists will have tremendous influence over what that legislation looks like."[9]

Over the coming years, activists will certainly continue to win many skirmishes. And, for sure, more people are likely to call for stricter controls on the technology. More citizens are likely to initiate – and win – legal challenges. More governments are likely to regulate the use of the technology, as Washington State has done. And more developers, retailers, and users are likely going to claim to be following ethical guidelines.

More jurisdictions, too, are likely to join San Francisco and Portland in banning the technology, and many more, particularly in liberal democracies, are likely to pass legislation to enhance civil rights and privacy protections. Before long, a few national governments may even end up implementing strict laws to control facial recognition technology. Still, the anti-FRT movement is going to need to build even larger coalitions, launch even more campaigns, and reach far deeper into the developing world to prevent facial recognition technology from becoming a normal feature of policing, surveillance, and everyday life for billions of people.

What does this conclusion suggest for our broader understanding of the power of activists to prevent the normalization of new technology?

THE POWER OF ACTIVISM TO RESIST NEW TECHNOLOGY

First and foremost, this book's analysis demonstrates the power of transnational social movements to delay, disrupt, and derail the uptake of new technology. They can clearly influence public opinion, shift societal norms, shame firms into shelving products, and persuade legislators to impose rules and bans. Still, any transnational social movement is best imagined as a patchwork of grassroots advocacy and formal organizations, replete with threadbare sections and gaping holes, and where individuals inevitably clash over priorities, tactics, and policies. Understanding the politics of transnational social movements in this way helps explain why so many states and firms are able to navigate around patches of intense local resistance. And it helps explain why activists have long struggled to prevent the globalization of new technology.

Resisting new technology, as the analysis in this book underscores, poses unique challenges for activists. Uptake of new technology tends to outpace scientific knowledge, public awareness, and policymaking processes. And this gap keeps growing as technological innovation accelerates. Governments, too, may intentionally delay or avoid regulating a new technology to gain strategic advantages, grow economies, or appease corporations.

Software technology is particularly difficult to campaign against on a global scale. Activists have no way of knowing how many startups are developing software in stealth mode. And these startups, which form and fail at a manic pace, may surface at any moment, from within any country, selling into markets all around the world. Before any alarm bells go off in the activist community, and with little accountability or transparency, governments, businesses, and schools can end up downloading software with questionable legal and ethical underpinnings. Resisting general-purpose software is particularly hard because it manifests in a great variety of applications, sometimes bringing grave dangers, but other times doing good.

The full consequences of any new technology, meanwhile, can take decades to emerge, well beyond the time horizons of activists, voters, and political parties. Adding to the challenge, new technology that functions as a source of power frequently diffuses through undemocratic corners of a state, as agencies deploy and repurpose the technology to extend authority and control. New surveillance technology is especially prone to diffusing through the backrooms of police forces, intelligence units, and militaries: a surveillance creep that is exceedingly hard to see, let alone stop.

As this book reveals, too, corporations pose yet another formidable challenge for activists trying to resist the normalization of technology. It is especially difficult to prevent small and medium-sized firms headquartered in emerging and developing countries from selling new technology. But transnational corporations, too, have long introduced new technology with little care or understanding of the social, political, or environmental consequences. This is true of the world's biggest oil, chemical, and automobile companies. It is the case for the weapons and pharmaceutical industries. It is true for logging, mining, and agricultural conglomerates. And it is the case for technology firms. Transnational corporations tend as well to overstate the value and understate the risks of profitable technology. Once a profitable technology is shown to be doing harm, moreover, they have a track record of deceiving publics, fighting phaseouts, and expanding sales in less regulated markets.[10]

Increasing the challenge for activists, the governance power of transnational corporations has been rising steadily over the past few decades.[11] The financial heft of the top firms now exceeds most states. Everywhere, meanwhile, governments have come to embrace corporate self-regulation as an effective and efficient way to govern new technology.[12] The refrain of CSR is helping activists to partner with firms like Google and Microsoft to lobby for controls on new technology. Not surprisingly, however, such lobbying tends to produce industry-friendly rules. Partnerships between nonprofits and businesses, moreover, are creating opportunities for firms to sow divisions within global activism, reinforcing cooperative, moderate NGOs and sidelining critical, radical groups.[13]

In short, extraordinarily powerful forces are propelling the normalization of new technology. Yet the arc of history would look very different without the layers of transnational social movements opposing technology. Militaries never did deploy blinding laser weapons in outer space. Firms and governments, too, have shelved technologies such as CFCs and leaded gasoline once the full consequences came to light. States have also reined in technologies after uprisings of civil society, including land mines, chemical weapons, biological weapons, and DDT (dichlorodiphenyltrichloroethane).[14] Granted, as this book reveals, stopping the global spread of a commercial, general-purpose digital technology poses an especially great challenge for activists. Even here, however, the politics of FRT demonstrates the power of activists to alter the reach, trajectory, and speed of uptake of a new technology.

Appendix: interviews

1. Brian Hofer, Executive Director of Secure Justice (US), December 1, 2021.
2. Anushka Jain, Associate Counsel, Internet Freedom Foundation (India), December 1, 2021.
3. Verónica Arroyo, Latin America Policy Analyst and Digital ID Policy Lead, Access Now (Peru), December 3, 2021.
4. Policy Analyst, Privacy Organization (US) (confidential interview), December 6, 2021.
5. Albert Fox Cahn, Executive Director of the Surveillance Technology Oversight Project (S.T.O.P) (US), December 8, 2021.
6. Pallavi Bedi, Centre for Internet and Society (India), December 9, 2021.
7. Jodie Siganto, Telecommunications and Internet Committee Chair (since 2021), the Australian Privacy Foundation (Australia), December 13, 2021.
8. Daniel Castro, Vice President of Information Technology and Innovation Foundation (US), December 13, 2021.
9. Tobias Urech, Campaigner, AlgorithmWatch (Switzerland), December 14, 2021.
10. Policy Analyst, Digital Rights Organization (Europe) (confidential interview), December 17, 2021.
11. Tracy Rosenberg, Executive Director at Media Alliance (US), December 17, 2021.
12. Kris Shrishak, Technology Fellow at the Irish Council for Civil Liberties (Ireland), December 20, 2021.
13. Yuri Guaiana, Senior Campaigns Manager at All Out (Italy), December 21, 2021.
14. Chérif El Kadhi, Middle East and North Africa Policy Analyst at Access Now (Tunisia), December 24, 2021.
15. Kade Crockford, Director of the Technology and Liberty Program at ACLU (US), January 4, 2022.

16. Nathan Freed Wessler, Deputy Director of the ACLU's Speech, Privacy, and Technology Project (US), January 11, 2022.
17. Calli Schroeder, Global Privacy Counsel at the Electronic Privacy Information Center (US), January 12, 2022.
18. Mike Katz-Lacabe, Director of Research at Oakland Privacy (US), January 12, 2022.
19. Daniel Leufer, Europe Policy Analyst at Access Now (Brussels), January 14, 2022.
20. Bryan Short, Digital Rights Campaigner at OpenMedia (Canada), January 14, 2022.
21. Laura Carrer, Digital Rights Unit, the Hermes Center for Transparency and Digital Human Rights (Italy), January 17, 2022.
22. Jennifer Jones, Staff Attorney, Technology and Civil Liberties Program, ACLU of Northern California (US), January 19, 2022.
23. Charlotte Burmeister, Digitale Freiheit (Germany), January 19, 2022.
24. Analyst and Campaigner, Privacy and Digital Rights Nonprofit (US) (confidential interview), January 21, 2022.
25. Alexandra Raphling, Chief of Staff at Encode Justice (US), January 25, 2022.
26. Emmanuelle Andrews, Policy and Campaigns Manager at Liberty (UK), January 26, 2022.
27. Caitlin Seeley George, Campaign Director, Fight for the Future (US), January 26, 2022.
28. Yuan Stevens, Legal Researcher (Canada), January 27, 2022.
29. Emily Roderick, Cofounder of The Dazzle Club (UK), January 27, 2022.
30. Hynek Trojánek, Public Relations Coordinator at the human rights NGO Iuridicum Remedium (IuRe) (Czech Republic), January 28, 2022.

Note: The University of British Columbia's Behavioural Research Ethics Board (certificate number, H21-03180) approved the methods, consent procedures, verification process, and data storage for these interviews.

Notes

1. INTRODUCING FACIAL RECOGNITION TECHNOLOGY

1. I am indebted to Rebecca Rogers for her outstanding research assistance and to the anonymous reviewers of this book for their astute feedback. A grant from the Social Sciences and Humanities Research Council of Canada supported the research for this book.
   Wang is quoted in Li Tao, "Jaywalkers Under Surveillance in Shenzhen Soon to be Punished Via Text Messages," *South Morning China Post*, March 27, 2018 (https://www.scmp.com).

2. Daniel Van Boom, "Chinese City Uses Surveillance Tech to Shame Citizens for Wearing Pajamas Outside," *CNET*, January 22, 2020 (https://www.cnet.com).

3. Li is quoted in Tony Bitzionis, "China Begins Testing Emotion Recognition Technology in Xinjiang Region," *Find Biometrics*, November 5, 2019 (https://findbiometrics.com).

4. CloudWalk is quoted in Paul Mozur, "Facial Scans Tighten China's Grip on a Minority," *New York Times*, April 15, 2019, p. A1.

5. Zhang is quoted in Nathan Vanderklippe, "Chinese School Installs Cameras to Monitor Students," *Globe and Mail*, June 2, 2018, p. A3.

6. See Appendix for a list of interviewees.

7. See, for instance, Erik Learned-Miller, Vicente Ordóñez, Jamie Morgenstern, and Joy Buolamwini, *Facial Recognition Technologies in the Wild: A Call for a Federal Office* (Algorithmic Justice League, 2020).

8. This definition is from Vermont General Assembly, "S.124 (Act 166), An Act Relating to Governmental Structures Protecting the Public Health, Safety and Welfare," October 7, 2020, available at https://legislature.vermont.gov/bill/status/2020/S.124.
   As I do in this book, legislation to ban or strictly limit FRT in the United States commonly treats "facial analysis" as a form of "facial recognition." Many organizations campaigning for bans on FRT, such as the Electronic Frontier Foundation, advocate for this definition of facial recognition. See, for instance, Bennett Cyphers, Adam Schwartz, and Nathan Sheard, "Face Recognition Isn't Just Face Identification and Verification: It's Also Photo Clustering, Race Analysis, Real-time Tracking, and More," *Electronic Frontier Foundation*, October 2, 2021 (https://www.eff.org).

Some analysts, however, think this is misleading and counterproductive, as facial analysis and facial recognition work differently, and each requires very different safeguards and policy measures. "Facial analysis and facial recognition are completely different in terms of the underlying technology and the data used to train them," argues Matt Wood of Amazon Web Services. "They may sound similar," adds Daniel Castro of the Information Technology and Innovation Foundation, "but they are as different as apple trees and apple sauce." See Matt Wood, "Thoughts on Recent Research Paper and Associated Article on Amazon Rekognition," *AWS Machine Learning Blog*, January 26, 2019 (https://aws.amazon.com); Daniel Castro, "Note to Press: Facial Analysis Is Not Facial Recognition," *Information Technology and Innovation Foundation: ITIF*, January 27, 2019 (https://itif.org). I am also grateful to Daniel Castro for explaining his reasoning during an interview on December 13, 2021.

9. Multiple interviewees, including Brian Hofer, Executive Director of Secure Justice (US), December 1, 2021; Verónica Arroyo, Latin America Policy Analyst and Digital ID Policy Lead, Access Now (Peru), December 3, 2021; Kris Shrishak, Technology Fellow at the Irish Council for Civil Liberties (Ireland), December 20, 2021; Yuri Guaiana, Senior Campaigns Manager at All Out (Italy), December 21, 2021; Nathan Freed Wessler, Deputy Director of the ACLU's Speech, Privacy, and Technology Project (US), January 11, 2022; Calli Schroeder, Global Privacy Counsel at the Electronic Privacy Information Center (US), January 12, 2022; Mike Katz-Lacabe, Director of Research at Oakland Privacy (US), January 12, 2022; Daniel Leufer, Europe Policy Analyst at Access Now (Brussels), January 14, 2022; Bryan Short, Digital Rights Campaigner at OpenMedia (Canada), January 14, 2022; Charlotte Burmeister, Digitale Freiheit (Germany), January 19, 2022; Emmanuelle Andrews, Policy and Campaigns Manager at Liberty (UK), January 26, 2022; Caitlin Seeley George, Campaign Director, Fight for the Future, January 26, 2022; Yuan Stevens, Legal Researcher (Canada), January 27, 2022; Emily Roderick, Cofounder of The Dazzle Club (UK), January 27, 2022.

10. Patrick Grother, Mei Ngan, and Kayee Hanaoka, *Face Recognition Vendor Test (FRVT) – Part III: Demographic Effects*, National Institute of Standards and Technology (NIST), US Department of Commerce, December 2019 (NISTIR 8280).

11. Stanley is quoted in Steven Melendez, "A Mass Study of 189 Face Recognition Algorithms Found Widespread Racial Bias 2019," *Fast Company*, December 19, 2019 (https://www.fastcompany.com).

12. Buolamwini is quoted in Harry de Quetteville, "Meet the Woman Fighting Racist, Sexist AI Algorithms – and Taking on the Tech Giants," *The Telegraph*, May 20, 2019 (https://www.telegraph.co.uk).

13. Jennifer Jones, Staff Attorney, Technology and Civil Liberties Program, ACLU of Northern California (US), January 19, 2022. Other interviewees made this point too, including Anushka Jain, Associate

Counsel, Internet Freedom Foundation (India), December 1, 2021, and Charlotte Burmeister, Digitale Freiheit (Germany), January 19, 2022.

[14.] Adam Schwartz, "Resisting the Menace of Face Recognition," *Electronic Frontier Foundation*, October 26, 2021 (https://www.eff .org).

[15.] Bedoya is quoted in Kate Conger, Richard Fausset, and Serge F. Kovaleski, "San Francisco Bans Facial Recognition Technology," *New York Times*, May 14, 2019.

[16.] Woodrow Hartzog and Evan Selinger, "Facial Recognition Is the Perfect Tool for Oppression," *Medium*, August 2, 2018 (https:// medium.com).

[17.] American Civil Liberties Union, Tweet, Twitter.com, May 22, 2019, available at https://twitter.com/ACLU/status/1131228523186802688.

[18.] I am grateful to the following interviewees for explaining the role of their organizations in opposing FRT: Anushka Jain, Associate Counsel, Internet Freedom Foundation (India), December 1, 2021; Verónica Arroyo, Latin America Policy Analyst and Digital ID Policy Lead, Access Now (Peru), December 3, 2021; Chérif El Kadhi, Middle East and North Africa Policy Analyst at Access Now (Tunisia), December 24, 2021; Kade Crockford, Director of the Technology and Liberty Program at ACLU (US), January 4, 2022; Nathan Freed Wessler, Deputy Director of the ACLU's Speech, Privacy, and Technology Project (US), January 11, 2022; Calli Schroeder, Global Privacy Counsel at the Electronic Privacy Information Center (US), January 12, 2022; Bryan Short, Digital Rights Campaigner at OpenMedia (Canada), January 14, 2022; Daniel Leufer, Europe Policy Analyst at Access Now (Brussels), January 14, 2022; Jennifer Jones, Staff Attorney, Technology and Civil Liberties Program, ACLU of Northern California (US), January 19, 2022; Emmanuelle Andrews, Policy and Campaigns Manager at Liberty (UK), January 26, 2022; Caitlin Seeley George, Campaign Director, Fight for the Future (US), January 26, 2022.

[19.] This assessment is based on the interviews listed in the Appendix. I am thankful to Emily Roderick of the Dazzle Club for explaining the role of artist-activists in opposing FRT (interview, January 27, 2022), Alexandra Raphling (interview, January 25, 2022) at Encode Justice for highlighting the importance of youth organizations, and Yuri Guaiana (interview, December 21, 2021) at All Out for underscoring the growing influence of LGBTQ+ organizations within the anti-FRT movement.

[20.] The Public Voice, "The Madrid Privacy Declaration: Global Privacy Standards for a Global World," November 3, 2009, available at https:// thepublicvoice.org/madrid-declaration, accessed May 9, 2022 (note: the 50th signature line is blank, leaving 111 signatories).

Mass surveillance involves general monitoring of a population. Examples include live facial recognition with surveillance cameras, police body cameras, and drones, as well as routine searching of facial databases to identify individuals from video footage or forensic sketches. This is in contrast to targeted surveillance, which is limited to a person, criminal gang, or terrorist cell. In jurisdictions with rule of law, targeted surveillance is generally done with probable cause and legal limits on scope and duration. Wiretapping is a common form of targeted surveillance.

21. Interviews with the ACLU's Kade Crockford (January 4, 2022), Nathan Freed Wessler (January 11, 2022), and Jennifer Jones (January 19, 2022).

22. Fight for the Future, Ban Facial Recognition, available at https://www.banfacialrecognition.com.

23. The Public Voice, "Declaration: A Moratorium on Facial Recognition Technology for Mass Surveillance Endorsements," October 2019, Tirana, Albania, accessed May 9, 2022 at https://thepublicvoice.org/ban-facial-recognition/endorsement. Note: The Declaration lists 114 signatories; however, Electronic Frontiers Australia and TCE Strategy (United States) are both listed twice.

24. ReclaimYourFace, "Reclaim Your Face Impact in 2021," December 21, 2021, available at https://reclaimyourface.eu/ryf-impact-2021.

25. See Fight for the Future, "Ban Facial Recognition in Stores," available at https://www.banfacialrecognition.com/stores.

26. See Amnesty International, "Ban the Scan," available at https://www.amnesty.org/en/petition/ban-the-scan-petition.

27. Interviews with Access Now's Verónica Arroyo (December 3, 2021), Chérif El Kadhi (December 24, 2021), and Daniel Leufer (January 14, 2022). See also Access Now, "Ban Biometric Surveillance," available at https://www.accessnow.org/ban-biometric-surveillance; Access Now, "Ban Automated Recognition of Gender and Sexual Orientation," available at https://act.accessnow.org/page/79916/action/1.

28. Big Brother Watch, "Stop Facial Recognition," available at https://bigbrotherwatch.org.uk/campaigns/stop-facial-recognition.

29. Interview, Anushka Jain (December 1, 2021); see also, Internet Freedom Foundation, "Project Panoptic," available at https://panoptic.in/about.

30. Interview, Bryan Short, Digital Rights Campaigner at OpenMedia (Canada), January 14, 2022; also see OpenMedia, "Ban Police Use of Facial Recognition in Canada," available at https://action.openmedia.org/page/63295/petition/1?locale=en-US.

31. Reclaim Your Face, Under the Tab "The Movement," available at https://reclaimyourface.eu. I am grateful to Hynek Trojánek at Iuridicum Remedium (IuRe) – a human rights NGO in the Czech Republic – for explaining the growing resistance to FRT in the Czech Republic (interview, January 28, 2022).

32. Interviews with Anushka Jain (December 1, 2021), Verónica Arroyo (December 3, 2021), Pallavi Bedi (December 9, 2021), and Chérif El Kadhi (December 24, 2021); also see Access Now, "Ban Biometric

Surveillance – Signers," updated December 21, 2021, accessed May 9, 2022 at https://www.accessnow.org/ban-biometric-surveillance.

2.   RESISTING THE NORMALIZATION OF FACIAL RECOGNITION

1.   Multiple interviewees listed in the Appendix emphasized the importance of the growing diversity of support for the rising power of the anti-FRT movement.

2.   Multiple interviewees, including Verónica Arroyo, Latin America Policy Analyst and Digital ID Policy Lead, Access Now (Peru), December 3, 2021.

3.   Multiple interviewees, including Anushka Jain, Associate Counsel, Internet Freedom Foundation (India), December 1, 2021; Kris Shrishak, Technology Fellow at the Irish Council for Civil Liberties (Ireland), December 20, 2021; Mike Katz-Lacabe, Director of Research at Oakland Privacy (US), January 12, 2022; Daniel Leufer, Europe Policy Analyst at Access Now (Brussels), January 14, 2022; Laura Carrer, Digital Rights Unit, the Hermes Center for Transparency and Digital Human Rights (Italy), January 17, 2022; Charlotte Burmeister, Digitale Freiheit (Germany), January 19, 2022; Jennifer Jones, Staff Attorney, Technology and Civil Liberties Program, ACLU of Northern California (US), January 19, 2022; Emmanuelle Andrews, Policy and Campaigns Manager at Liberty (UK), January 26, 2022; Yuan Stevens, Legal Researcher (Canada), January 27, 2022.

4.   As Verónica Arroyo (December 3, 2021) noted when interviewed for this book, "a moratorium is just delaying the problem."

5.   Based on interviews listed in the Appendix.

6.   Interview, Tracy Rosenberg, Executive Director at Media Alliance (US), December 17, 2021.

7.   This assessment of the rising support for outright bans on the use of FRT by governments and private businesses is based on the interviews listed in the Appendix.

8.   Access Now, "Ban Biometric Surveillance – Signers," updated December 21, 2021, accessed May 9, 2022 at https://www.accessnow .org/ban-biometric-surveillance.

9.   This assessment is based on interviews listed in the Appendix.

10.   European Parliament, "European Parliament Resolution of 6 October 2021 on Artificial Intelligence in Criminal Law and Its Use by the Police and Judicial Authorities in Criminal Matters," adopted October 6, 2021, text available at https://www.europarl.europa.eu/doceo/ document/TA-9-2021-0405_EN.html.

11.   European Digital Rights (EDRi), "New German Government Calls for European Ban on Biometric Mass Surveillance," *EDRi*, December 1, 2021 (https://edri.org).

12. European Data Protection Supervisor, "EDPB & EDPS Call for Ban on Use of AI for Automated Recognition of Human Features in Publicly Accessible Spaces," *EDPS Press Release*, June 21, 2021 (https://edps .europa.eu). See also Melissa Heikkilä, "AI: Decoded: UNESCO's AI Ethics Framework," *Politico*, November 24, 2021 (https://www .politico.eu).

13. United Nations High Commissioner for Human Rights, *The Right to Privacy in a Digital Age*. Submitted to the UN Human Rights Council, September 13, 2021, p. 12.

14. Interview, Caitlin Seeley George, Campaign Director, Fight for the Future, January 26, 2022.

15. I am grateful to Emmanuelle Andrews, Policy and Campaigns Manager at Liberty (UK), for clarifying and verifying this information (by email correspondence, April 28, 2022). For details, see Liberty, "Legal Challenge: Ed Bridges v South Wales Police," available at https:// www.libertyhumanrights.org.uk/issue/legal-challenge-ed-bridges-v -south-wales-police (accessed May 9, 2022).

16. Interviews with Anushka Jain, Associate Counsel, Internet Freedom Foundation (India), December 1, 2021; Pallavi Bedi, Centre for Internet and Society (India), December 9, 2021.

17. To justify crackdowns and delegitimize dissent, governments around the world are increasingly describing activists as "agents of foreign influence." See Miriam Matejova, Stefan Parker, and Peter Dauvergne, "The Politics of Repressing Environmentalists as Agents of Foreign Influence," *Australian Journal of International Affairs* 72 (2) (2018): 145–62.

18. See the Appendix for a list of interviewees.

19. Kelly A. Gates, *Our Biometric Future: Facial Recognition Technology and the Culture of Surveillance* (New York University Press, 2011).

20. See, for example, David Lyon, *The Culture of Surveillance* (Polity, 2018); Shoshana Zuboff, *The Age of Surveillance Capitalism: The Fight for a Human Future at the New Frontier of Power* (Public Affairs, 2018).

21. See, for instance, Bernard Keenan, "Automatic Facial Recognition and the Intensification of Police Surveillance," *The Modern Law Review* 84 (4) (2021): 886–97; Thiago Guimarães Moraes, Eduarda Costa Almeida, and José Renato Laranjeira de Pereira, "Smile, You Are Being Identified! Risks and Measures for the Use of Facial Recognition in (Semi-)Public Spaces," *AI and Ethics* 1 (2021): 159–72; Sarah Moulds, "Who's Watching the 'Eyes'? Parliamentary Scrutiny of National Identity Matching Laws," *Alternative Law Journal* 45 (4) (2020): 266–9.

22. Sandro Galea, "Making the Case for a World Without Guns," *The Lancet Public Health* 4 (6) (2019): e266–e267; Aaron Karp, *Estimating Global Civilian-Held Firearms Numbers* (Small Arms Survey, Briefing Paper, June 2018).

23. Kelly A. Clancy, *The Politics of Genetically Modified Organisms in the United States and Europe* (Palgrave Macmillan, 2017).

24. Matthew Paterson, *Automobile Politics: Ecology and Cultural Political Economy* (Cambridge University Press, 2007).

25. See, for example, Brett Frischmann and Evan Selinger, *Re-Engineering Humanity* (Cambridge University Press, 2018); Bert-Jaap Koops, "The Concept of Function Creep," *Law, Innovation and Technology* 13 (1) (2021): 29–56; Beatriz da Costa, Jamie Schulte, and Brooke Singer, "Surveillance Creep! New Manifestations of Data Surveillance at the Beginning of the Twenty-First Century," *Radical History Review* 95 (Spring 2006): 70–88.

3.   THE MOVEMENT TO OPPOSE FACIAL RECOGNITION

1. Wheeler is quoted in Rachel Metz, "Portland Passes Broadest Facial Recognition Ban in the United States," *CNN Business*, September 9, 2020 (https://edition.cnn.com). The 2020 Portland City Council FRT ordinances do allow residents to unlock a personal iPad or iPhone with face recognition. Residents can also continue to have a facial recognition doorbell or home security system. In addition, there are a few exceptions where businesses can still use the technology (e.g., when necessary to comply with US federal or state laws).

2. Wheeler is quoted in Alfred Ng, "Portland, Oregon, Passes Toughest Ban on Facial Recognition in US," *CNET*, September 10, 2020 (https://www.cnet.com).

3. Carson is quoted in Taylor Hatmaker, "Portland Passes Expansive City Ban on Facial Recognition Tech," *TechCrunch*, September 9, 2020 (https://techcrunch.com).

4. Holland is quoted in Jonathan Greig, "Portland Becomes First City to Ban Companies from Using Facial Recognition Software in Public," *TechRepublic*, September 14, 2020 (https://www.techrepublic.com). A confidential interview in January 2022 with a campaigner in Portland, Oregon, also informs my understanding of the politics of resistance to FRT in Portland.

5. See, for example, Craig M. Kauffman and Pamela L. Martin, *The Politics of Rights of Nature: Strategies for Building a More Sustainable Future* (MIT Press, 2021); Robin Broad and John Cavanagh, *The Water Defenders: How Ordinary People Saved a Country from Corporate Greed* (Beacon Press, 2021); Craig M. Kauffman, *Grassroots Global Governance: Local Watershed Management Experiments and the Evolution of Sustainable Development* (Oxford University Press, 2016).

6. This assessment is partly based on interviews listed in the Appendix.

7. This assessment is partly based on interviews listed in the Appendix.

8. Evan Selinger and Woodrow Hartzog, "Amazon Needs to Stop Providing Facial Recognition Tech for the Government," *Medium*, June 21, 2018 (https://medium.com).

9. Interview, Jennifer Jones, Staff Attorney, Technology and Civil Liberties Program, ACLU of Northern California, January 19, 2022.

10. Woodrow Hartzog and Evan Selinger, "Facial Recognition Is the Perfect Tool for Oppression," *Medium*, August 2, 2018 (https://medium.com). See also Evan Selinger and Woodrow Hartzog, "The Inconsentability of Facial Surveillance," *Loyola Law Review* 66 (2019): 101–22.

11. Luke Stark, "Facial Recognition is the Plutonium of AI," *XRDS* 25 (3) (Spring 2019): 50, 52.

12. ACLU, "The Fight to Stop Face Recognition Technology," *ACLU*, July 15, 2021 (https://www.aclu.org/news/topic/stopping-face-recognition-surveillance).

13. Electronic Frontier Foundation, "About Face," accessed May 9, 2022 at https://www.eff.org/aboutface.

14. Hayes's remarks are posted on the website for US Congresswoman Ayanna Pressley: "Reps. Pressley, Jayapal, Tlaib, Clarke & Sens. Markey, Merkley Announce Legislation to Ban Government Use of Facial Recognition, Other Biometric Technology," *Press Release*, June 25, 2020 (https://pressley.house.gov/media/press-releases).

15. Hooper is quoted in Melissa Hellmann, "Advocacy Group Launches National Campaign to Ban Facial-Recognition Technology from Government Use," *PHYS.ORG*, July 9, 2019 (https://phys.org). For a similar viewpoint, see Melinda Sebastian, "Normalizing Resistance: Saying No to Facial Recognition Technology," *Feminist Media Studies* 20 (4) (2020): 594–7.

16. Fitzgerald's remarks are in Ed Markey, "Senators Markey and Merkley, and Reps. Jayapal, Pressley to Introduce Legislation to Ban Government Use of Facial Recognition, Other Biometric Technology," *Markey Press Release*, June 25, 2020 (https://www.markey.senate.gov).

17. Amnesty International USA, "As Global Protests Continue, Facial Recognition Technology Must Be Banned," *Amnesty International News*, June 11, 2020 (https://www.amnesty.org/en).

18. International Civil Liberties Monitoring Group, Letter to The Honourable Bill Blair, Minister of Public Safety and Emergency Preparedness, July 8, 2020, available at https://iclmg.ca/wp-content/uploads/2020/07/facial-recognition-letter-08072020.pdf.

19. Liberty, "Resist Facial Recognition," accessed May 9, 2022 at https://www.libertyhumanrights.org.uk/campaign/resist-facial-recognition.

20. Greer is quoted in Makena Kelly, "Feds Would Be Banned from Using Facial Recognition Under New Bill," *The Verge*, June 25, 2020 (https://www.theverge.com).

21. Ban Facial Recognition, available at https://www.banfacialrecognition.com. See also Fight for the Future, available at https://www.fightforthefuture.org/about.

22. Access Now, "Open Letter Calling for a Global Ban on Biometric Recognition Technologies that Enable Mass and Discriminatory Surveillance," June 7, 2021, available at https://www.accessnow.org/cms/assets/uploads/2021/06/BanBS-Statement-English.pdf.

23. Access Now, "Ban Biometric Surveillance – Signers," updated December 21, 2021, accessed May 9, 2022 at https://www.accessnow.org/ban-biometric-surveillance.

24. Daniel Castro, "NO: Despite the Cries of Alarm, the Technology Is Mostly Beneficial", *Wall Street Journal*, February 24, 2020.

25. Beltrá is quoted in "AI-Enabled Facial Recognition: More Than Just Ethics?" The Presidency Debates, YouTube video, June 7, 2019, at www.youtube.com/watch?v=A-h0MAxj_fI.

26. Based on interviews in December 2021 and January 2022 with campaigners opposing FRT (see Appendix).

27. Based on interviews in December 2021 and January 2022 with campaigners opposing FRT (see Appendix).

28. Vatican, "Rome Call for AI Ethics," Rome, February 28, 2020, p. 6.

29. Multiple interviewees, including Tracy Rosenberg, Executive Director at Media Alliance, December 17, 2021; Kade Crockford, Director of the Technology and Liberty Program at ACLU, January 4, 2022; Mike Katz-Lacabe, Director of Research at Oakland Privacy (US), January 12, 2022; Jennifer Jones, Staff Attorney, Technology and Civil Liberties Program, ACLU of Northern California, January 19, 2022; Caitlin Seeley George, Campaign Director, Fight for the Future, January 26, 2022; and a policy analyst with a US privacy organization (confidential interview, December 6, 2021).

30. Bill Radke and Alison Bruzek, "Microsoft President Brad Smith on Consumer Privacy," transcript of Bill Radke's interview of Brad Smith, KUOW and NPR, January 16, 2020 (https://www.kuow.org).

31. Brad Smith, "Facial Recognition: It's Time for Action," *Microsoft on the Issues, the Official Microsoft Blog*, December 6, 2018 (https://blogs.microsoft.com).

32. Based on interviews listed in the Appendix.

33. Based on interviews listed in the Appendix.

34. This assessment is partially based on interviews listed in the Appendix.

35. Open Letter to Elijah Cummings and Jim Jordan of the US House Oversight and Reform Committee, June 3, 2019, available at https://www.aclu.org/letter/coalition-letter-calling-federal-moratorium-face-recognition.

36. The Public Voice, "Declaration: A Moratorium on Facial Recognition Technology for Mass Surveillance Endorsements," accessed May 9, 2022 at https://thepublicvoice.org/ban-facial-recognition/endorsement.

37. See "Ban Facial Recognition," Electronic Privacy Information Center (EPIC), available at https://epic.org/banfacesurveillance.

38. This assessment draws on the interviews in the Appendix.

39. The Public Voice, "Declaration: A Moratorium on Facial Recognition Technology for Mass Surveillance Endorsements."

40. Interviews with Anushka Jain, Associate Counsel, Internet Freedom Foundation (India), December 1, 2021; Pallavi Bedi, Centre for Internet and Society (India), December 9, 2021.

41. Based on multiple interviewees, including Anushka Jain, December 1, 2021; Pallavi Bedi, December 9, 2021; Verónica Arroyo, Latin America Policy Analyst and Digital ID Policy Lead, Access Now (Peru), December 3, 2021; Chérif El Kadhi, Middle East and North Africa Policy Analyst at Access Now (Tunisia), December 24, 2021.

42. Access Now, "Ban Biometric Surveillance – Signers," updated December 21, 2021, accessed May 9, 2022 at https://www.accessnow .org/ban-biometric-surveillance.

4.   THE POLITICS OF FACIAL RECOGNITION BANS IN THE UNITED STATES

1. These high school students are quoted in Davey Alba, "Facial Recognition Moves into a New Front: Schools," *New York Times*, February 6, 2020.

2. Shultz is quoted in Erin Durkin, "New York School District's Facial Recognition System Sparks Privacy Fears," *Guardian*, May 31, 2019.

3. Coyle is quoted in Alba, "Facial Recognition Moves into a New Front."

4. See Jim Shultz, "Time for Change in Lockport School Board," *Union-Sun & Journal*, May 23, 2020 (https://www.lockportjournal .com); Connor Hoffman, "Renee Cheatham Wins a Seat on the School Board," *Union-Sun & Journal*, June 18, 2020 (https://www .lockportjournal.com).

5. Coyle is quoted in Taylor Hatmaker, "New York Legislature Votes to Halt Facial Recognition Tech in Schools for Two Years," *TechCrunch*, July 23, 2020 (https://techcrunch.com).

6. City and County of San Francisco, Administrative Code – Acquisition of Surveillance Technology, Amended in Committee May 6, 2019, Ordinance, file number, 190110, pp. 2, 11.

7. Clare Garvie, Alvaro M. Bedoya, and Jonathan Frankle, *The Perpetual Line-Up: Unregulated Police Face Recognition in America*, Center on Privacy & Technology at Georgetown Law, October 18, 2016 (https:// www.flawedfacedata.com).

8. San Francisco has a long history of contrarian activism to resist mainstream thinking, corporate power, and state authority. For one example, see Jason Henderson, *Street Fight: The Politics of Mobility in San Francisco* (University of Massachusetts Press, 2013).

9. See ACLU of Northern California et al., "Letter to the San Francisco Board of Supervisors in Support of the Stop Secret Surveillance Ordinance," April 9, 2019, available at https://src.bna.com/H8Y.

10. I am grateful to Brian Hofer for explaining his role in the San Francisco campaign during an interview on December 1, 2021.

11. American Civil Liberties Union of Northern California, "San Francisco Board of Supervisors Approves Historic Face Surveillance Ban and Oversight Law," Media Release, May 14, 2019.

12. Cagle is quoted in Kate Conger, "The Man Behind San Francisco's Facial Recognition Ban," *New York Times*, May 15, 2019.

13. Peskin is quoted in Kate Conger, Richard Fausset, and Serge F. Kovaleski, "San Francisco Bans Facial Recognition Technology," *New York Times*, May 14, 2019.

14. Turley is quoted in Conger, Fausset, and Kovaleski.

15. Castro is quoted in Kartikay Mehrotra, "San Francisco Bans City Use of Facial-Recognition Tech Tools," *Bloomberg Wire Service*, May 14, 2019 (https://www.bloomberg.com).

16. Daniel Castro, "The Case for Facial Recognition," *Government Technology* (April/May) 2019, p. 9. Daniel Castro elaborated on his case for facial recognition during an interview on December 13, 2021.

17. Gregory Barber, "San Francisco Bans Agency Use of Facial-Recognition Tech," *Wired*, May 14, 2019 (https://www.wired.com).

18. IBIA is quoted in "San Francisco Residents Question City's Facial Recognition Ban," *Biometric Technology Today*, June 2019, p. 1.

19. Stop Crime SF, "Open Letter to San Francisco Board of Supervisors," *Stop Crime SF: Neighbourhoods for Criminal Justice Accountability*, March 29, 2019, available at https://stopcrimesf.com/blog/2019/4/11/video-surveillance-legislation-needs-re-thinking.

20. Engardio is quoted in Conger, Fausset, and Kovaleski. See also Stop Crime SF, "Statement on San Francisco's Ban of Facial Recognition Technology," *Stop Crime SF: Neighborhoods for Criminal Justice Accountability*, May 14, 2019, available at https://stopcrimesf.com/blog/2019/5/14/statement-on-san-franciscos-ban-of-facial-recognition-technology.

21. For the 2020 amendment banning facial recognition technology, see Cambridge, Massachusetts, *Code of Ordinances*, Chapter 2.128 – Surveillance Technology Ordinance, 2.128.075 – Prohibition on City's Acquisition and/or Use of Face Recognition Technology.

22. McGovern is quoted in Stefan Geller, "Cambridge City Council Bans Face Surveillance Technology," *Boston Herald*, January 14, 2020 (https://www.bostonherald.com).

23. Crockford is quoted in ACLU Massachusetts, "Cambridge Passes Municipal Ban on Face Surveillance Technology," *ACLU Massachusetts News*, January 13, 2020 (https://www.aclum.org).

24. Stamps is quoted in Kayode Crown, "Jackson Bans Facial Recognition Tech; New Airport Academy, Sewer Repairs," *Jackson Free Press*, August 20, 2020 (https://www.jacksonfreepress.com).

25. Schilling is quoted in ACLU of Vermont, "ACLU of Vermont Statement on the Enactment of S.124, the Nation's Strongest Statewide Ban on Law Enforcement Use of Facial Recognition Technology," *ACLU of Vermont*, October 8, 2020 (https://www.acluvt.org). Except for drones, Vermont's bill imposes a "moratorium" on facial recognition technology until the state's General Assembly authorizes usage. As the ACLU of Vermont says, this is in effect an "outright ban" because the legislation does not include a timeline or establish a process for considering possible regulations. See Vermont General Assembly, "S.124 (Act 166), An Act Relating to Governmental Structures Protecting the Public Health, Safety and Welfare," October 7, 2020, available at https://legislature.vermont.gov/bill/status/2020/S.124.

26. Jackson Cote, "Who's Watching You?" *MassLive.com*, February 2, 2020 (updated February 27, 2020) (https://www.masslive.com).

27. ACLU of Massachusetts, "Face Surveillance Moratorium: An Act Establishing a Moratorium on Face Recognition and Other Biometric Surveillance Systems, S.1385 & H.1538 | Sen. Cynthia Creem and Rep. David Rogers," ACLU of Massachusetts Information Sheet, 2019, available at https://www.aclum.org/en/legislation/face-surveillance-moratorium.

28. Commonwealth of Massachusetts (191st General Court), "An Act Establishing a Moratorium on Face Recognition and Other Remote Biometric Surveillance Systems," Bill S.1385, Senate Docket, No. 671, filed on January 15, 2019 (https://malegislature.gov) (for the bill's history, see https://malegislature.gov/Bills/191/S1385/BillHistory).

29. Creem is quoted in Steve LeBlanc, "Moratorium Urged on Use of Facial Recognition Technology," *AP News*, June 22, 2019 (https://apnews.com).

30. Robert Winterton (Director of Public Affairs at NetChoice), "Tell Massachusetts Politicians to Let Police Use New Law Enforcement Tech," *Change.org*, petition started in 2019 (https://www.change.org).

31. See Jake Parker, "Why SIA Opposes Massachusetts' Far-Reaching Facial Recognition Technology Prohibition Bill," *Security Industry Association*, October 28, 2019 (https://www.securityindustry.org).

32. International Biometrics + Identity Association (IBIA), *Comments from IBIA on MA S.1385 and MA H.1538: Legislation Proposing to Place a Moratorium on Facial Recognition Technology*, IBIA, November 4, 2019 (https://www.ibia.org).

33. Tarr and Leahy are quoted in Christian M. Wade, "Massachusetts Bill Puts Limits on Facial Scan Technology," *gt: government technology*, December 3, 2020 (https://www.govtech.com).

34. The Commonwealth of Massachusetts (191st General Court), "An Act Relative to Justice, Equity and Accountability in Law Enforcement in the Commonwealth," Bill No. 2963, Senate, December 1, 2020.

35. Baker is quoted in Matt Stout, "Baker Sends Police Bill Back to Legislature, Asking for Changes," *The Boston Globe*, December 10, 2020 (https://www.bostonglobe.com).

36. "Rep. Pressley's Statement on Gov. Baker's Amendments to Police Reform Bill," *Press Release*, US Congresswoman Ayanna Pressley, Serving the 7th District of Massachusetts, December 11, 2020 (https://pressley.house.gov).

37. ACLU Massachusetts, "Statement of ACLU on Governor Baker Amendment Cutting Face Surveillance Regulations," *News Statement*, December 10, 2020 (https://www.aclum.org).

38. Quoted in Conor Roche, "Celtics Players Call for Gov. Baker to End Facial Recognition Surveillance," *The Boston Globe*, December 16, 2020 (https://www.boston.com).

39. The Commonwealth of Massachusetts (191st General Court), Bill No. 2981, Senate, December 21, 2020.

40. Brownsberger is quoted in Chris Lipinski, "Senate Votes for Police Reform Changes in Compromise with Baker," *State House News Service*, December 21, 2020 (https://statehousenews.com).

41. Carol Rose, Rahsaan Hall, and Kade Crockford, "What the Movement for Police Accountability Achieved in 2020 – And What Comes Next," *ACLU Massachusetts*, January 4, 2021 (https://www.aclum.org).

42. González and Chrispin are quoted in "Governor Baker Signs Police Reform Legislation," *Press Release*, Office of Governor Charlie Baker and Lt. Governor Karyn Polito, December 31, 2020 (https://www.mass.gov).

43. Senators Ed Markey and Jeff Merkley and Representatives Pramila Jayapal and Ayanna Pressley introduced the bill in June 2020, titled "The Facial Recognition and Biometric Technology Moratorium Act of 2020."

44. The remarks of Merkley, Markey, and Pressley are in Ed Markey, "Senators Markey and Merkley, and Reps. Jayapal, Pressley to Introduce Legislation to Ban Government Use of Facial Recognition, Other Biometric Technology," *Markey Press Release*, June 25, 2020 (https://www.markey.senate.gov).

45. The remarks of Collins-Dexter, Guliani, and Greer are in Markey, "Senators Markey and Merkley."

46. AI Now Institute, *AI Now 2019 Report*, December 2019, p. 6. Kate Crawford codirects the AI Now Institute.

47. AI Now Institute, *AI Now 2018 Report*, December 2018, p. 4. For an example of research claiming that facial recognition technology can identify political orientation, see Michal Kosinski, "Facial Recognition Technology Can Expose Political Orientation from Naturalistic Facial Images," *Scientific Reports* 11 (1) (2021), available at https://doi.org/10.1038/s41598-020-79310-1.

48. See, for instance, ACLU, "Nationwide Coalition of Over 85 Groups Urges Companies Commit Not to Provide Face Surveillance to the

Government," *ACLU Press Release*, January 15, 2019 (https://www
.aclu.org).

49.   See Google AI, "Artificial Intelligence at Google: Our Principles,"
available at https://ai.google/principles.

50.   IBM, "IBM CEO's Letter to Congress on Racial Justice Reform," *IBM
ThinkPolicy Blog*, June 8, 2020 (https://www.ibm.com); the quote
"a history of human rights abuses" is from IBM, "IBM Response to
'BIS Notice of Inquiry on Advanced Surveillance Systems and Other
Items of Human Rights Concern'," September 11, 2020, available at
https://www.ibm.com/blogs/policy/wp-content/uploads/2020/09/IBM
-comments-to-BIS-September-11-2020.pdf.

51.   The Axon statement is quoted in Kate Crawford, "Regulate
Facial-Recognition Technology," *Nature* 572 (August 29, 2019): 565.

52.   Open letter to the Axon AI Ethics Board, April 26, 2018, posted on the
website for The Leadership Conference on Civil and Human Rights,
available at https://civilrights.org/resource/axon-product-development
-law-enforcement. In 2019, Axon's AI and Policing Technology
Ethics Board recommended against the company using facial recognition technology. See Axon Enterprise, *First Report of the Axon AI &
Policing Technology Ethics Board*, June 2019.

53.   Daniel E. Bromberg, Étienne Charbonneau, and Andrew Smith,
"Public Support for Facial Recognition via Police Body-Worn
Cameras: Findings from a List Experiment," *Government Information
Quarterly* 37 (1) (2020): 101415.

54.   Dave Gershgorn, "Exclusive: Live Facial Recognition Is Coming to
U.S. Police Body Cameras," *OneZero*, March 4, 2020 (https://onezero
.medium.com).

55.   The FBI was reportedly averaging more than 4,000 facial recognition
searches a month in 2019. See Drew Harwell, "FBI, ICE Find State
Driver's License Photos are a Gold Mine for Facial-Recognition
Searches," *Washington Post*, July 7, 2019.

56.   Markey is quoted in Alexandra S. Levine, "Clearview AI On Track
to Win U.S. Patent for Facial Recognition Technology," *Politico*,
December 4, 2021 (https://www.politico.com).

57.   Garvie, Bedoya, and Frankle, p. 1.

5.   REGULATING FACIAL RECOGNITION IN THE UNITED STATES

1.   For an insightful profile of Senator Joe Nguyen, see Rich Smith, "Joe
Nguyen is an AOC of the Washington Senate," *The Stranger*, April 9,
2019 (https://www.thestranger.com).

2.   Nguyen is quoted in "Senate Passes Nguyen Bill to Regulate Facial
Recognition Technology," *State Democrats* (Media Releases),
February 19, 2020 (http://sdc.wastateleg.org).

3. Nguyen is quoted in "Governor Signs Facial Recognition Regulations into Law," *State Democrats* (Media Releases), March 31, 2020 (http://sdc.wastateleg.org).

4. See *Certification of Enrollment Engrossed Substitute Senate Bill 6280*, 66th Legislature 2020 Regular Session, March 12, 2020, p. 11.

5. See *Certification of Enrollment Engrossed Substitute Senate Bill 6280*. For a timeline of the bill, see Washington State Bill Information, SB 6280 – 2019–20, Concerning the Use of Facial Recognition Services, Washington State Legislature (https://app.leg.wa.gov).

6. Jamie Davies, "Microsoft Praises Facial Recognition Regulation Progress," *Telecoms*, April 2, 2020 (https://telecoms.com).

7. Brad Smith, "Finally, Progress on Regulating Facial Recognition," *Microsoft on the Issues* (the official Microsoft blog), March 31, 2020 (https://blogs.microsoft.com).

8. At the time of writing in 2022, Senator Nguyen was a senior program manager at Microsoft.

9. Brad Smith, "Facial Recognition Technology: The Need for Public Regulation and Corporate Responsibility," *Microsoft on the Issues* (the official Microsoft blog), July 13, 2018 (https://blogs.microsoft.com).

10. See Microsoft, "Responsible AI," available at https://www.microsoft.com/en-us/ai/responsible-ai.

11. Ajay Agrawal, Joshua Gans, and Avi Goldfarb, *Prediction Machines: The Simple Economics of Artificial Intelligence* (Harvard Business Review Press, 2018); Thomas H. Davenport, *The AI Advantage: How to Put the Artificial Intelligence Revolution to Work* (MIT Press, 2018).

12. Smith made these comments during an interview on *Washington Post Live*, "The Path Forward: Technology & Society," June 11, 2020, available on Twitter at https://twitter.com/i/broadcasts/1OdKrWPnzXnGX. In this interview, he confirmed that his company was not currently selling facial recognition software to US police departments. He did not say, however, whether or not Microsoft was supplying software to other US law enforcement agencies or foreign police departments, although he did mention that Microsoft's human rights guidelines did not allow his company to sell facial recognition technology to China. The company did not respond to calls by the ACLU to clarify Smith's statements.

13. Smith, "Finally, Progress on Regulating Facial Recognition."

14. Jennifer Lee, "We Need a Face Surveillance Moratorium, Not Weak Regulations: Concerns about SB 6280," *ACLU Washington*, March 31, 2020 (https://www.aclu-wa.org).

15. Lee, "We Need a Face Surveillance Moratorium."

16. Dave Gershgorn, "A Microsoft Employee Literally Wrote Washington's Facial Recognition Law," *OneZero*, April 2, 2020 (https://onezero.medium.com).

17. Mehreen Kasana, "A Microsoft Employee Penned Washington State's Sketchy Facial Recognition Law," *Input*, April 3, 2020 (https://

www.inputmag.com). Multiple interviewees were similarly critical of Washington State's facial recognition regulation, including Kade Crockford, Director of the Technology and Liberty Program at ACLU (US), January 4, 2022, and Caitlin Seeley George, Campaign Director, Fight for the Future (US), January 26, 2022.

18. Raybould is quoted in Tracy Ryan, "Washington State OKs Facial Recognition Law Seen as National Model," *Wall Street Journal*, March 31, 2020 (https://www.wsj.com).

19. Microsoft's statement is in Assembly Bill Policy Committee Analysis (AB 2261, as introduced February 14, 2020), Assembly Committee on Privacy and Consumer Protection, Ed Chau, Chair. Date of Hearing: May 5, 2020. For the proposed bill, see Assembly Bill No. 2261, introduced by Assembly Member Chau, California legislature – 2019–20 regular session, February 14, 2020.

20. The coalition statement is in Assembly Bill Policy Committee Analysis (AB 2261, as introduced February 14, 2020).

21. See Michelle Goodwin et al., Letter to the Honorable Ed Chau, May 1, 2020, available at https://www.aclunc.org/sites/default/files/2020.05 .01%20-%20Public-health%20letter%20FINAL.pdf.

22. See, for instance, Information Technology and Innovation Foundation, Testimony of Daniel Castro, Vice President, Information Technology and Innovation Foundation Before the House Committee on Oversight and Reform Hearing on "Facial Recognition Technology (Part III): Ensuring Commercial Transparency & Accuracy," January 15, 2020, available at https://docs.house.gov/meetings/GO/GO00/20200115/ 110380/HHRG-116-GO00-Wstate-CastroD-20200115.pdf.

23. Cahn is quoted in Alfred Ng, "Facial Recognition's Fate Could Be Decided in 2021," *CNET*, December 11, 2020 (https://www.cnet .com). I am grateful to Albert Fox Cahn for elaborating on his analysis of the politics of the globalization of FRT (interview, December 8, 2021).

24. Carl Szabo, "Industry Group Launches Defense of Facial Recognition Technology," *NetChoice Press Release*, October 9, 2019 (https:// netchoice.org).

25. Nine organizations and associations signed the letter: Airports Council International – North America; American Association of Airport Executives; Consumer Technology Association; Global Business Travel Association; Identification Technology Association; International Biometrics + Identity Association; NetChoice; Security Industry Association; and the US Chamber of Commerce. The letter is posted online at US Chamber of Commerce, "Coalition Letter on Facial Recognition Technology," October 16, 2019 at https://www .uschamber.com/letters-congress/coalition-letter-facial-recognition -technology.

26. Day is quoted in Adam Janofsky, "Business Groups Push Back Against Proposed Facial-Recognition Bans," *Wall Street Journal*, October 30, 2019 (https://www.wsj.com).

27. Michael Punke, "Some Thoughts on Facial Recognition Legislation," *AWS Machine Learning Blog*, February 7, 2019 (https://aws.amazon .com).

28. "Letter from Nationwide Coalition to Amazon CEO Jeff Bezos Regarding Rekognition," June 18, 2018, copy uploaded to the website of the American Civil Liberties Union (https://www.aclu.org).

29. Amazon, "We Are Implementing a One-Year Moratorium on Police Use of Rekognition," *The Amazon Blog*, June 10, 2020 (https://blog .aboutamazon.com).

30. Jeffrey Dastin, "Amazon Extends Moratorium on Police Use of Facial Recognition Software," *Reuters*, May 18, 2021 (https://www.reuters .com).

31. Gomez's letter is reprinted in Rachel Uranga, "Congressman Slams Amazon's Use of Facial Recognition Technology, Calls for New Disclosures," *GeekWire*, June 17, 2020 (https://www.geekwire.com).

32. Microsoft President Brad Smith made this commitment on June 11, 2020, during a livestream session with the *Washington Post*. At the time, it should be noted, the company was not supplying facial recognition software to US police forces.

33. Some of the world's leading suppliers of facial recognition technology did push back against calls to end sales to US police forces. Japan's NEC Corporation, for instance, said it is confident the technology can "correct inherent biases, protect privacy and civil liberties, and fairly and effectively conduct investigations for social justice." NEC is quoted in Geoffrey A. Fowler, "Black Lives Matter Could Change Facial Recognition Forever – If Big Tech Doesn't Stand in the Way," *Washington Post Blogs*, June 12, 2020 (https://www.washingtonpost .com).

34. O'Sullivan and Spivack are quoted in Fowler, "Black Lives Matter Could Change Facial Recognition Forever." Multiple interviewees listed in the Appendix made similar remarks about the motives and objectives underlying Microsoft's FRT lobbying.

35. This assessment is based on multiple interviewees listed in the Appendix.

6. RISING GLOBAL OPPOSITION TO FACE SURVEILLANCE

1. The Public Voice, "Declaration: A Moratorium on Facial Recognition Technology for Mass Surveillance Endorsements," accessed May 9, 2022, available at https://thepublicvoice.org/ban-facial-recognition/ endorsement.

2. Electronic Frontier Foundation, "About Face," available at http://www .eff.org/aboutface.

3. Katitza Rodriguez, "Activists Worldwide Face Off Against Face Recognition: 2019 Year in Review," *Electronic Frontier Foundation*, December 30, 2019 (https://www.eff.org).

4. Based on 30 interviews in December 2021, and January 2022, with FRT experts and activists (see Appendix).

5. See Freedom House, *Freedom in the World 2022: The Global Expansion of Authoritarian Rule* (Freedom House, February 2022) and Global Freedom Scores, available at https://freedomhouse.org/countries/freedom-world/scores.

6. For a list of signatories to the Albania Declaration, see the Public Voice, "Declaration."

7. See ACLU, "Nationwide Coalition of Over 85 Groups Urges Companies Commit Not to Provide Face Surveillance to the Government," *ACLU Press Release*, January 15, 2019 (https://www.aclu.org).

8. The Fight for the Future open letter is available for signing at Parents Against Facial Recognition at https://www.parentsagainstfacialr ecognition.org.

9. One example is the open letter to Elijah Cummings and Jim Jordan of the US House Oversight and Reform Committee, June 3, 2019 (https://www.aclu.org/letter/coalition-letter-calling-federal-moratorium-face -recognition).

10. International Civil Liberties Monitoring Group, Letter to The Honourable Bill Blair, Minister of Public Safety and Emergency Preparedness, July 8, 2020, available at https://iclmg.ca/wp-content/uploads/2020/07/facial-recognition-letter-08072020.pdf.

11. European Digital Rights (EDRi) (lead authors Ella Jakubowska and Diego Naranjo), *Ban Biometric Mass Surveillance: A Set of Fundamental Rights Demands for the European Commission and EU Member States* (EDRi, 2020), p. 4.

12. See Reclaim Your Face (https://reclaimyourface.eu). The campaign was launched in November 2020.

13. Big Brother Watch, "Joint Statement on Police and Private Company Use of Facial Recognition Surveillance in the UK," September 2019, available on the Big Brother Watch website (https://bigbrotherwatch .org.uk).

14. One example is the Human Rights, Big Data and Technology Project at the University of Essex's Human Rights Centre (https://www.hrbdt .ac.uk). Another example is the Ada Lovelace Institute, which is supported by the UK's Nuffield Foundation (https://www.adalovelac einstitute.org).

15. Equality and Human Rights Commission (EHRC), "Facial Recognition Technology and Predictive Policing Algorithms Out-Pacing the Law," *EHRC Press Release*, March 12, 2020 (https://www .equalityhumanrights.com).

16. Justice Sub-Committee on Policing, the Scottish Parliament, *Facial Recognition: How Policing in Scotland Makes Use of This Technology*, SP Paper 678, 1st Report, 2020 (Session 5), February 11, 2020, p. 1.

17. Finnie is quoted in *BBC*, "Facial Recognition: 'No Justification' for Police Scotland to Use Technology," *BBC News*, February 11, 2020 (https://www.bbc.com). Police Scotland has shelved plans to deploy live facial recognition technology by 2026; however, this police force does use what the subcommittee calls "retrospective facial recognition technology."

18. La Quadrature du Net, "Joint Letter from 80 Organisations: Ban Security and Surveillance Facial Recognition," La Quadrature du Net, December 19, 2019 (https://www.laquadrature.ne).

19. Philipp Grüll (translated by Daniel Eck), "Germany's Plans for Automatic Facial Recognition Meet Fierce Criticism," *EURACTIV. de*, January 1, 2020 (updated January 15, 2020) (https://www.euractiv .com).

20. See Roskomsvoboda, "Campaign Against Racial Recognition," available at https://bancam.ru/en.

21. Marcus Hoy, "Police Use of Facial Recognition Tech Approved in Sweden," *Bloomberg Law*, October 25, 2019 (https://news .bloomberglaw.com).

22. Bert Peeters, "Facial Recognition at Brussels Airport: Face Down in the Mud," *Ku Leuven and CiTip Blog* (Centre for IT & IP Law), March 17, 2020 (https://www.law.kuleuven.be).

23. Laura Carrer, Riccardo Coluccini, and Philip Di Salvo, "How Facial Recognition Is Spreading in Italy: The Case of Como," *Privacy International* (Case Study), September 17, 2020 (https:// privacyinternational.org). I am grateful to Laura Carrer for providing background on the anti-FRT campaign in Italy (interview, January 17, 2022).

24. See GDPR.EU, "Complete Guide to GDPR Compliance," available at https://gdpr.eu.

25. Muselie is quoted in Laura Kayali, "French Privacy Watchdog Says Facial Recognition Trial in High Schools is Illegal," *Politico*, October 29, 2019 (updated October 30, 2019) (https://www.politico.eu).

26. EU Charter of Fundamental Rights, Title II, Freedoms, Article 8 – Protection of Personal Data, available at https://fra.europa.eu/en/eu -charter/article/8-protection-personal-data.

27. Samuel Stolton, "LEAK: Commission Considers Facial Recognition Ban in AI 'White' Paper," *EURACTIV*, January 16, 2020 (updated January 21, 2020) (https://www.euractiv.com).

28. European Union Agency for Fundamental Rights (FRA), *Facial Recognition Technology: Fundamental Rights Considerations in the Context of Law Enforcement* (FRA, 2019), p. 34.

29. Carly Kind, "Nowhere to Hide," *The World Today*, February and March 2020 (a Chatham House publication, available at https://www .chathamhouse.org). Carly Kind is the director of the London-based Ada Lovelace Institute.

30. Kate Saslow, "EU is 'Wild West' Compared to US on Facial Recognition Rules," *Euobserver*, June 26, 2020 (https://euobserver.com).

31. Janosch Delcker and Cristiano Lima, "Fight Against Facial Recognition Hits a Wall Across the West," *Politico*, December 27, 2019 (updated December 31, 2019) (https://www.politico.eu).

32. Interviews with Anushka Jain, Associate Counsel, Internet Freedom Foundation (India), December 1, 2021; Verónica Arroyo, Policy Analyst, Access Now (Peru), December 3, 2021; Pallavi Bedi, Centre for Internet and Society (India), December 9, 2021; Chérif El Kadhi, Middle East and North Africa Policy Analyst at Access Now (Tunisia), December 24, 2021.

33. Access Now, "Ban Biometric Surveillance – Signers," updated December 21, 2021, accessed May 9, 2022 at https://www.accessnow.org/ban-biometric-surveillance.

34. Maria Laura Canineu, "High-Tech Surveillance: From China to Brazil?" *Human Rights Watch*, May 31, 2019 (https://www.hrw.org).

35. The American company AdMobilize provided the facial analysis system.

36. An English-language copy of the expert opinion is available on the Access Now website at https://www.accessnow.org/cms/assets/uploads/2020/06/Expert_Opinion_Brazil_Facial_Categorization.pdf.

37. Arroyo is quoted in Access Now, "Data for Sale in Brazil: Access Now Files Expert Opinion in São Paulo Metro Facial Recognition Case," June 24, 2020 (https://www.accessnow.org). I am grateful to Verónica Arroyo for explaining the growing strength of the anti-FRT movement in Latin America (interview, December 3, 2021).

38. This surveillance system searches a database of "fugitives," from those accused of petty theft to those wanted for murder. See ADC at https://adc.org.ar/en; also, Dave Gershgorn, "The U.S. Fears Live Facial Recognition. In Buenos Aires, It's a Fact of Life," *OneZero*, March 3, 2020 (https://onezero.medium.com).

39. TEDIC, "Who Watches the Watchman? Facial Recognition in Asunción," September 16, 2019 (https://www.tedic.org/en).

40. Interviews with Anushka Jain (December 1, 2021) and Pallavi Bedi (December 9, 2021).

41. Gupta is quoted in Eoin Higgins, "'An Act of Mass Surveillance': India Use of Facial Recognition Tech Against Protesters Angers Privacy Advocates," *The Independent*, December 31, 2019. See also Internet Freedom Foundation, "Facial Recognition," available at https://internetfreedom.in/tag/facial-recognition.

42. Interview with Anushka Jain (December 1, 2021).

43. Amnesty International, "Amnesty International Calls for Ban on the Use of Facial Recognition Technology for Mass Surveillance," *Amnesty International Blog*, June 11, 2020 (https://www.amnesty.org).

44. Wang is quoted in Edd Gent, "Concerns Raised Over India's Facial Recognition Plan," *New Scientist* 244 (3260), December 14, 2019, p. 9.

45. Chris Burt, "Morocco Extends Facial Recognition Moratorium to Year-End, Proposes Biometric Authentication Service," *BiometricUpdate.com*, April 9, 2020 (https://www.biometricupdate .com).

46. Lia Holland at Fight for the Future made the comment about hoping to "beat back" FRT, as quoted in Chapter 3.

7. THE CORPORATE POLITICS OF FACIAL RECOGNITION

1. Allied Market Research (authored by Beesetty Yogendra, Shadaab Khan, Pramod Borasi, and Vineet Kumar), *Global Facial Recognition Market: Opportunities and Forecasts, 2021–2030* (Allied Market Research, February 2022).

2. Kashmir Hill, "The Secretive Company That Might End Privacy as We Know It," *New York Times*, January 18, 2020.

3. For an overview of Clearview AI's ties to the far-right, see Luke O'Brien, "The Far-Right Helped Create the World's Most Powerful Facial Recognition Technology," *HuffPost*, April 7, 2020 (updated April 9, 2020) (https://www.huffingtonpost.com).

4. Stilgherrian, "Victoria Police Emails Reveal Clearview AI's Dodgy Direct Marketing", *ZDNet*, June 21, 2020 (https://www.zdnet.com).

5. See Ryan Mac, Caroline Haskins, and Logan McDonald, "Clearview's Facial Recognition App Has Been Used by the Justice Department, ICE, Macy's, Walmart, and the NBA," *BuzzFeed News*, February 27, 2020 (https://www.buzzfeednews.com).

6. Ferrara is quoted in Hill, "The Secretive Company."

7. Ton-That is quoted in Hill, "The Secretive Company."

8. US Senator Ron Wyden, January 19, 2020 (https://twitter.com/ RonWyden).

9. Garvie is quoted in Mac, Haskins, and McDonald, "Clearview's Facial Recognition App."

10. Greer is quoted in Mac, Haskins, and McDonald, "Clearview's Facial Recognition App."

11. Ton-That is quoted in Hill, "The Secretive Company."

12. The Illinois Biometric Information Privacy Act requires businesses to obtain opt-in consent to collect, store, or disclose an individual's faceprint, and empowers individuals to sue violators.

13. Wessler is quoted in Ryan Mac, Caroline Haskins, and Logan McDonald, "Clearview AI Has Promised to Cancel All Relationships with Private Companies," *BuzzFeed News*, May 7, 2020 (https://www .buzzfeednews.com). I am grateful to Nathan Wessler for elaborating on his concerns with Clearview AI's practices (interview, January

11, 2022). Multiple interviewees similarly condemned Clearview AI's business model, including Anushka Jain, Associate Counsel, Internet Freedom Foundation (India), December 1, 2021; Brian Hofer, Executive Director of Secure Justice (US), December 1, 2021; Verónica Arroyo, Latin America Policy Analyst and Digital ID Policy Lead, Access Now (Peru), December 3, 2021; Tracy Rosenberg, Executive Director at Media Alliance (US), December 17, 2021; Calli Schroeder, Global Privacy Counsel at the Electronic Privacy Information Center (US), January 12, 2022; Mike Katz-Lacabe, Director of Research at Oakland Privacy (US), January 12, 2022; Bryan Short, Digital Rights Campaigner at OpenMedia (Canada), January 14, 2022; Caitlin Seeley George, Campaign Director, Fight for the Future (US), January 26, 2022.

[14.] European Data Protection Board (EDPD), "Response to MEPs on Use of Clearview AI by Law Enforcement Authorities," *EDPD News*, June 10, 2020 (https://edpb.europa.eu).

[15.] Office of the Privacy Commissioner of Canada, "Clearview AI Ceases Offering Its Facial Recognition Technology in Canada," *News Release*, July 6, 2020 (https://www.priv.gc.ca). After nearly a year-long investigation, Canada's national privacy commissioner, Daniel Therrien, was pointed in his conclusion: "What Clearview does is mass surveillance, and it is illegal." Therrien is quoted in Office of the Privacy Commissioner of Canada, "Clearview AI's Unlawful Practices Represented Mass Surveillance of Canadians, Commissioners Say," *Press Release*, February 3, 2021 (https://www.priv.gc.ca).

[16.] UK Information Commissioner's Office, "The Office of the Australian Information Commissioner and the UK's Information Commissioner's Office Open Joint Investigation into Clearview AI Inc.," *Statement*, July 9, 2020 (https://ico.org.uk).

[17.] Alessandro Mascellino, "Italian Privacy Authority Fines Clearview AI €20M, Orders Biometrics Deletion," *Biometric Update.com*, March 11, 2022 (http://www.biometricupdate.com).

[18.] The quote "solve thousands of serious crimes" is from Clearview AI, "Clearview Is Not a Consumer Application," *Clearview AI Blog*, January 23, 2020 (https://blog.clearview.ai).

[19.] Kim Lyons, "ICE Just Signed a Contract with Facial Recognition Company Clearview AI," *The Verge*, August 14, 2020 (https://www.theverge.com).

[20.] Tyler Choi, "Clearview Facial Recognition App Up to 20B Images," *BiometricUpdate.com*, March 28, 2022 (https://www.biometricupdate.com).

[21.] Quoted in Drew Harwell, "Ukraine Is Scanning Faces of Dead Russians, Then Contacting the Mothers," *Washington Post*, April 15, 2022 (https://www.washingtonpost.com) (the quote is from a financial presentation by Clearview AI in December 2021).

22. Jared Council, "Local Police Force Uses Facial Recognition to Identify Capitol Riot Suspects," *Wall Street Journal*, January 8, 2021 (https://www.wsj.com); Kashmir Hill, "The Facial-Recognition App Clearview Sees a Spike in Use After Capitol Attack," *New York Times*, January 9, 2021 (https://www.nytimes.com).

23. Harwell, "Ukraine Is Scanning Faces of Dead Russians."

24. "Controversial Tech Company Pitches Facial Recognition to Track COVID-19," *NBC News NOW*, April 27, 2020, available at https://twitter.com/NBCNewsNow/status/1254924882934185984.

25. Jerome Pesenti, "An Update on Our Use of Face Recognition," *Meta Newsroom*, November 2, 2021, available at https://about.fb.com/news/2021/11/update-on-use-of-face-recognition.

26. See National Institute of Standards and Technology (NIST), *The Face Recognition Vendor Test 2018*, National Institute of Standards and Technology, US Department of Commerce, 2018, available at https://pages.nist.gov/frvt/html/frvt1N.html.

27. Chris Gallagher, "Masks No Obstacle for New NEC Facial Recognition System," *U.S. News and World Report*, January 7, 2021 (https://www.usnews.com).

28. See Metropolitan Police, "Live Facial Recognition," accessed May 9, 2022 at https://www.met.police.uk/advice/advice-and-information/fr/facial-recognition.

29. Dave Gershgorn, "From RealPlayer to Toshiba, Tech Companies Cash in on the Facial Recognition Gold Rush," *OneZero*, June 2, 2020 (https://onezero.medium.com).

30. See Thales at https://www.thalesgroup.com.

31. Gartner (lead author Nick Ingelbrecht), *Market Trends: Facial Recognition for Enhanced Physical Security – Differentiating the Good, the Bad and the Ugly* (Gartner, April 5, 2019); Gershgorn, "From RealPlayer to Toshiba."

32. See Ayonix (https://ayonix.com); Cognitec (https://www.cognitec.com); and iOmniscient (https://iomni.ai).

33. Kanga and Vural are quoted in Julia Horowitz, "Tech Companies Are Still Helping Police Scan Your Faces," *CNN Business*, July 3, 2020 (https://www.cnn.com).

34. See NtechLab at https://ntechlab.com.

35. FIFA stands for Fédération Internationale de Football Association.

36. Sobyanin is quoted in James Vincent, "Moscow Rolls Out Live Facial Recognition System with an App to Alert Police," *The Verge*, January 30, 2020 (https://www.theverge.com).

37. FindFace, "Public Safety with FindFace," available at https://findface.pro/en/solution/public-safety.

38. Carly Kind, "Nowhere to Hide," *The World Today*, February and March 2020 (a Chatham House publication, available at https://www.chathamhouse.org); see also the market analysis: IHS Markit (https://ihsmarkit.com).

39. Steven Feldstein, *The Global Expansion of AI Surveillance* (Carnegie Endowment for International Peace, 2019), pp. 25–8.

40. Steven Feldstein, "The Road to Digital Unfreedom: How Artificial Intelligence is Reshaping Repression," *Journal of Democracy* 30 (1) (2019): 40–52.

41. Anna Gross, Madhumita Murgia, and Yuan Yang, "Chinese Tech Groups Shaping UN Facial Recognition Standards," *Financial Times*, December 1, 2019 (https://www.ft.com).

42. See Sarah Biddulph, *Handbook on Human Rights in China* (Edward Elgar Publishing, 2019).

43. Paul Mozur, Jonah M. Kessel, and Melissa Chan, "Made in China, Exported to the World: The Surveillance State," *New York Times*, April 24, 2019.

8. THE EVERYDAY POLITICS OF FACIAL RECOGNITION IN CHINA

1. The park spokesperson is quoted in "Beijing Park Dispenses Loo Roll Using Facial Recognition," *BBC*, March 20, 2017 (https://www.bbc.com) (first quoted in Beijing Wanbao – in English, the *Beijing Evening News*).

2. Wang is quoted in Javier C. Hernández, "China's High-Tech Tool to Fight Toilet Paper Bandits," *New York Times*, March 20, 2017.

3. Zhang, Wu, and Liu are quoted in A. J. Willingham and Nanlin Fang, "Chinese Park Installs Facial Recognition Software to Stop Toilet Paper Thieves," *CNN*, March 21, 2017 (https://www.cnn.com).

4. Masha Borak, "China's Public Toilets Now Have Facial Recognition, Thanks to Xi Jinping," *Tech in Asia*, December 20, 2018 (https://www.techinasia.com); Jenny Lin, "The Curious Case of Toilet Paper and Facial Recognition," *UX Collective*, March 17, 2019 (https://uxdesign.cc).

5. Alex Linder, "Facial Recognition Toilet Paper Dispenser Rolled Out at Shanghai Public Bathroom!" *Shanghaiist*, June 8, 2018 (http://shanghaiist.com).

6. Paul Bischoff, "Surveillance Camera Statistics: Which Cities Have the Most CCTV Cameras?" *Comparitech*, updated May 17, 2021 (http://www.comparitech.com). (The projection for the total number of surveillance cameras in China relies on market analysis by IHS Markit at https://ihsmarkit.com.)

7. James Leibold, "Surveillance in China's Xinjiang Region: Ethnic Sorting, Coercion, and Inducement," *Journal of Contemporary China* 29 (121) (2020): 46–60.

8. Paul Mozur, Jonah M. Kessel, and Melissa Chan, "Made in China, Exported to the World: The Surveillance State," *New York Times*, April 24, 2019.

9. Until making headlines in 2020, Alibaba's Chinese-language website for cloud computing was claiming its facial recognition security service could detect "sensitive people" in pictures and videos, including Uyghurs. The English-language marketing did not contain this information. See IPVM Team, "Alibaba Uyghur Recognition as a Service," *IPVM*, December 16, 2020 (https://ipvm.com); Raymond Zhong, "As China Tracked Muslims, Alibaba Showed Customers How They Could, Too," *New York Times*, December 16, 2020 (updated December 17, 2020).

10. Jane Li, "Shanghai Apartment Buildings Are Secretly Installing Facial Recognition Devices," *Quartz*, October 18, 2019 (https://qz.com).

11. Quoted in Xinhua, "Facial Recognition Piloted in Beijing's Public Rental Housing," *XinhuaNet*, March 9, 2019 (https://www.xinhuanet.com/english).

12. The Nandu Personal Information Protection Research Center conducted this survey online in October and November of 2019 (with 6,152 respondents). For a summary, see Sam Shead, "Chinese Residents Worry About Rise of Facial Recognition," *BBC*, December 5, 2019 (https://www.bbc.com/news).

13. See Genia Kostka, Léa Steinacker, and Miriam Meckel, "Between Security and Convenience: Facial Recognition Technology in the Eyes of Citizens in China, Germany, the United Kingdom, and the United States," *Public Understanding of Science* 30 (6) (2021): 679–80.

14. See Shead, "Chinese Residents Worry About Rise of Facial Recognition."

15. The Weibo and Ou Biaofeng quotes are in Joyce Huang, "Chinese Citizens Express Concern Over the Abuse of Facial Recognition Technology," *VOA*, December 3, 2019 (https://www.voanews.com).

16. Wang and the Chengdu resident are quoted in Lily Kuo, "'The New Normal': China's Excessive Coronavirus Public Monitoring Could Be Here to Stay," *Guardian*, March 9, 2020 (https://www.theguardian.com).

17. Carolyn L. Hsu, "The Rise of NGOs in the People's Republic of China," *Handbook of Research on NGOs* (Edward Elgar Publishing, 2018), pp. 368–90; Margaret E. Roberts, *Censored: Distraction and Diversion Inside China's Great Firewall* (Princeton University Press, 2018).

18. Wang Yiqing, "Face-Recognition Technology Reunited More Than 10,000 Lost People," *The Straits Times*, January 21, 2020 (https://www.straitstimes.com).

19. Newsflare, "Chinese Pupils Scan Faces at Facial Recognition Gate to Enter School," a video shot in Shenzhen in Guangdong Province, June 12, 2019, posted at www.dailymotion.com/video/x7bhvn4.

20. Quoted in "East China University Tests Facial Recognition in Classrooms, Dismisses Students' Concerns," *Global Times*, September 2, 2019 (https://www.globaltimes.cn).

21. "Is Facial Recognition Technology Being Abused in Classrooms?" *Beijing Review*, September 26, 2019 (a collection of newspaper editorials debating the use of facial recognition technology in schools in China) (http://www.bjreview.com); Ran Yu, "No Place for 'Surveillance' Cameras in Class," *ChinaDaily.com.cn*, September 7, 2019 (https://global.chinadaily.com.cn).

22. Cao is quoted in Siyi Zhang, "Schools Using Facial Recognition System Sparks Privacy Concerns in China," *jmdedu*, September 9, 2019 (https://en.jmdedu.com).

23. Xinmei Shen, "China is Putting Surveillance Cameras in Plenty of Schools," *Tech in Asia*, January 22, 2019 (https://www.techinasia.com).

24. Xu is quoted in GETChina Insights, "Schools Using Facial Recognition System Sparks Privacy Concerns in China," *Medium*, September 9, 2019 (https://medium.com).

25. GETChina Insights, "Schools Using Facial Recognition System."

26. These students are quoted in Cate Cadell and Gabriel Crossley, "Facial Recognition and Bathtime Bookings: How China's Universities Are Reopening," *Reuters*, August 31, 2020 (https://www.reuters.com).

27. Ding Yi, "Trending in China: Tencent Uses Facial Recognition to Fight Gaming Addiction – Cue Happy and Angry Faces," *Caixin*, June 19, 2020.

28. Professor Ouyang is interviewed in the video "Buying Food with Facial Recognition in China," January 2, 2019, available at https://www.youtube.com/watch?v=9HHW0mj2EDc.

29. Huang Ge and Xu Keyue, "Hangzhou Safari Park Goes to Court in China's First Facial Recognition-Related Litigation," *Global Times*, November 3, 2019 (https://www.globaltimes.cn).

30. Eva Dou, "China Built the World's Largest Facial Recognition System. Now, It's Getting Camera-Shy," *The Washington Post*, July 30, 2021.

31. Yuan Ye, "A Professor, A Zoo, and the Future of Facial Recognition in China," *Sixth Tone*, April 26, 2021 (http://www.sixthtone.com).

9. THE GLOBALIZATION OF FACIAL RECOGNITION TECHNOLOGY

1. Harrisburg University of Science and Technology, "HU Facial Recognition Software Predicts Criminality," *Harrisburg University Press Release*, May 5, 2020. Following a storm of controversy, the university deleted this press release, saying the researchers were "updating the paper to address concerns raised." The original announcement can still be viewed in the internet archives at https://archive.is/N1HVe #selection-1601.0-1601.140.

2. Ferguson is quoted in A. J. Dellinger, "A Twisted Project That Tried to Predict Criminals from a Photo Has Come to an End," *Mic*, June 24, 2020 (https://www.mic.com).

3. Korn is quoted in Harrisburg University of Science and Technology, "HU Facial Recognition Software Predicts Criminality."

4. Figols is quoted in "Manchester City and Brondby Have Turned to Blink Identity and Panasonic for Facial Recognition Technology," *Biometric Technology Today*, September 2019, p. 3.

5. Patrick Grother, Mei Ngan, and Kayee Hanaoka, *Ongoing Face Recognition Vendor Test (FRVT) Part 2: Identification* (National Institute of Standards and Technology, US Department of Commerce, November 2018), p. 2.

6. The Japanese police officer is quoted in Alessandro Mascellino, "Police in Japan Reveal Use of Facial Biometrics in Criminal Probes," *Biometric Update.com*, September 16, 2020 (https://www.biometricupdate.com).

7. Wong is quoted in Zhaki Abdullah, "Privacy, Data Security Concerns as Facial Recognition Becomes More Common," *Channel News cana* (CNA), November 18, 2019 (https://www.channelnewsasia.com).

8. Chow Kon Yeow is quoted in Opalyn Mok, "Penang Launches Country's First Facial Recognition CCTV Surveillance," *Malay Mail*, January 2, 2019.

9. Krishan is quoted in Rahimi Yunus and Asila Jalil, "Facial Recognition Tech Grows Amid Concerns," *The Malaysian Reserve*, December 5, 2019.

10. Soibam Rocky Singh, "Facial Recognition Technology: Law Yet to Catch Up," *The Hindu*, December 31, 2020 (http://www.thehindu.com).

11. Jay Mazoomdaar, "Delhi Police Film Protests, Run Its Images Through Face Recognition Software to Screen Crowd," *The Indian Express*, December 28, 2019.

12. Shah is quoted in Manish Singh, "India Used Facial Recognition to Identify 1,100 Individuals at a Recent Riot," *TechCrunch*, March 11, 2020.

13. Interview with Jodie Siganto, Telecommunications and Internet Committee Chair (since 2021), the Australian Privacy Foundation (Australia), December 13, 2021.

14. See Jake Goldenfein and Monique Mann, "Australian Identity-Matching Services Bill," in Amba Kak, ed., *Regulating Biometrics: Global Approaches and Urgent Questions* (AI Now Institute, September 1, 2020), pp. 44–51.

15. LoopLearn's website is http://www.looplearn.net.

16. Kathryn Steele, "Delta Expands Optional Facial Recognition Boarding to New Airports, More Customers," *Delta News Hub*, December 8, 2019, available at https://news.delta.com/delta-expands-optional -facial-recognition-boarding-new-airports-more-customers.

17. US Department of Homeland Security, *Fiscal Year 2018 Entry/Exit Overstay Report* (Homeland Security, 2019), p. 4.
18. Summarized in Tom Simonite, "Facial Recognition Is Being Banned – But It's Still Everywhere," *Wired*, December 22, 2021, available at https://www.wired.com/story/face-recognition-banned-but-everywhere.
19. Dave Gershgorn, "Airports Are Normalizing Facial Recognition in the United States," *OneZero*, December 18, 2019 (https://onezero.medium.com).
20. Parmy Olson, "Facial Recognition's Next Big Play: The Sports Stadium," *The Wall Street Journal*, August 1, 2020 (https://www.wsj.com); Dave Clark, "Mets to Expand Facial Recognition System to All Entry Gates in 2022," *Ticket News*, December 10, 2021, at https://www.ticketnews.com/2021/12/mets-to-expand-facial-recognition-system-to-all-entry-gates-in-2022.
21. See Mark Andrejevic and Neil Selwyn, "Facial Recognition Technology in Schools: Critical Questions and Concerns," *Learning, Media and Technology* 45(2) (2020): 115–28; Lucas Ropek, "Facial Recognition Software on the Rise in U.S. Schools," *gt: government technology*, June 29, 2020 (http://www.govtech.com).
22. The estimate of enrollment in the Texas City Independent School District is from the US National Center for Education Statistics for the year 2018–19.
23. Cavness is quoted in Tom Simonite and Gregory Barber, "The Delicate Ethics of Using Facial Recognition in Schools," *Wired*, October 17, 2019 (http://www.wired.com).
24. The quote "you meet superior firepower with superior firepower" is in Simonite and Barber, "The Delicate Ethics of Using Facial Recognition in Schools." The quote "it just makes the fight fair" is in Diane Ritchey, "Setting the Gold Standard in School Security," *Security: Solutions for Enabling and Assuring Business*, March 1, 2020 (https://www.securitymagazine.com).
25. Matranga is quoted in Simonite and Barber, "The Delicate Ethics of Using Facial Recognition in Schools."
26. The quote "you have surveillance cameras at Disney World" is in Simonite and Barber, "The Delicate Ethics of Using Facial Recognition in Schools." The quote "people need to stop being so sensitive" is in Chris Stewart, "Texas School District Invests in High-Tech Security Software to Protect Students," *Denver7*, February 14, 2020 (http://www.thedenverchannel.com).
27. Glaser is quoted in Simonite and Barber, "The Delicate Ethics of Using Facial Recognition in Schools."
28. Lee is quoted at SAFR for Security at https://safr.com/security.
29. The staff member is quoted in Steven Melendez, "Yes, RealNetworks Still Exists, and Now It's Selling Face Surveillance," *Fast Company*, April 9, 2019 (http://www.fastcompany.com).

30. Glaser is quoted in "RealNetworks Offers Facial Recognition to Secure Schools from Shooters," *Biometric Technology Today* (September) (2018), p. 1.

31. Cusick is quoted in Issie Lapowsky, "Schools Can Now Get Facial Recognition Tech for Free. Should They?" *Wired*, July 17, 2018 (https://www.wired.com).

32. Etzioni is quoted in Rachel Lerman, "As Facial-Recognition Technology Grows, So Does Wariness about Privacy. Use at a School in Seattle Fuels Debate," *The Seattle Times*, September 28, 2018 (updated September 29, 2018) (https://www.seattletimes.com).

33. See Metropolitan Police, "Live Facial Recognition," accessed May 9, 2022 at https://www.met.police.uk/advice/advice-and-information/fr/facial-recognition.

34. Big Brother Watch Team, "Facial Recognition 'Epidemic' in the UK," *Big Brother Watch*, August 16, 2019, available at https://bigbrotherwatch.org.uk/2019/08/facial-recognition-epidemic-in-the-uk.

35. Nicolas Kayser-Bril, "At Least 11 Police Forces Use Face Recognition in the EU AlgorithmWatch Reveals," *AlgorithmWatch*, December 11, 2019 (updated June 18, 2020) (https://algorithmwatch.org).

36. Rosbach is quoted in Joe Pinkstone, "Russia's 'Most Popular Search Engine' Yandex Is Branded 'Creepy' After Tests Reveal It Uses Facial Recognition to Reveal Identities in Anonymous Images," *Daily Mail*, January 16, 2020 (https://www.dailymail.co.uk).

37. Steven Feldstein, *The Global Expansion of AI Surveillance* (Carnegie Endowment for International Peace, 2019), pp. 25–8.

38. Stephen Kafeero, "Uganda is Using Huawei's Facial Recognition Tech to Crack Down on Dissent after Anti-Government Protests," *Quartz Africa*, November 27, 2020 (https://qz.com).

39. Turinawe is quoted in Elias Biryabarema, "Ugandan Police Say CCTV System Will Cut Crime, But Citizens Are Sceptical," *Business Day*, August 15, 2019 (http://www.businesslive.co.za).

40. Quoted in Chris Burt, "Chinese Biometric Surveillance Technology Deployed Internationally Amid Criticism," *Biometric Update.com*, October 23, 2019 (http://www.biometricupdate.com).

41. Sophie Foggin, "Will This Be the Last Time Brazil Uses Facial Recognition Technology at Carnival?" *The Sociable*, March 2, 2020 (https://sociable.co).

42. Mariana Canto, "We Don't Need No Observation: The Use and Regulation of Facial Recognition in Brazilian Public Schools," *Global Information Society Watch*, 2019 (http://www.giswatch.org).

43. José Miguel Vivanco, "Letter to Buenos Aires Mayor Horacio Rodríguez Larreta Re: Facial Recognition System and Children's Rights," *Human Rights Watch*, October 9, 2020 (https://www.hrw.org).

44. See Vivanco, "Letter to Buenos Aires Mayor."

45. Enonchong is quoted in Tony Bitzionis, "Biometric Facial Recognition Solution Focused on African Faces Wins Acclaim," *CNET*, September 9, 2020 (https://www.cnet.com).

46. Paul Bischoff, "Facial Recognition Technology (FRT): 100 Countries Analyzed," *Comparitech*, June 8, 2021 (https://www.comparitech.com). North Korea was not included in the analysis because of lack of data.

47. Bischoff, "Facial Recognition Technology."

48. Bischoff, "Facial Recognition Technology."

10. THE FUTURE OF FACIAL RECOGNITION TECHNOLOGY

1. This assessment draws on the interviews listed in the Appendix, including Anushka Jain (December 1, 2021), Verónica Arroyo (December 3, 2021), Tobias Urech (December 14, 2021), Pallavi Bedi (December 9, 2021), Albert Fox Cahn (December 8, 2021), Kris Shrishak (December 20, 2021), Jodie Siganto (December 13, 2021), Yuri Guaiana (December 21, 2021), Chérif El Kadhi (December 24, 2021), Kade Crockford (January 4, 2022), Calli Schroeder (January 12, 2022), Mike Katz-Lacabe (January 12, 2022), Daniel Leufer (January 14, 2022), Laura Carrer (January 17, 2022), Charlotte Burmeister (January 19, 2022), Emmanuelle Andrews (January 26, 2022), Yuan Stevens (January 27, 2022), Hynek Trojánek (January 28, 2022), and confidential interviews with analysts at privacy and digital rights organizations on December 17, 2021 and January 21, 2022.

2. Based on multiple interviewees listed in the Appendix.

3. Fight for the Future, "Ban Facial Recognition in Stores," available at https://www.banfacialrecognition.com/stores.

4. Interview, Yuri Guaiana, Senior Campaigns Manager at All Out (Italy), December 21, 2021; for the Access Now campaign, see Access Now, "Ban Automated Recognition of Gender and Sexual Orientation," available at https://act.accessnow.org/page/79916/action/1.

5. Global Witness, *Last Line of Defence* (Global Witness, 2021).

6. See Ban Facial Recognition, accessed May 9, 2022 at https://www.banfacialrecognition.com; Greenpeace USA, "Tell Amazon: Stop Selling Racist Tech," accessed May 9, 2022 at https://engage.us.greenpeace.org/24xw-IESMkaq3pyM-fn9pw2.

7. The Extinction Rebellion (Philippines), for instance, signed a 2021 open letter calling for a ban on biometric surveillance. See Access Now, "Ban Biometric Surveillance – Signers," updated December 21, 2021, accessed May 9, 2022 at https://www.accessnow.org/ban-biometric-surveillance.

8. Peter Dauvergne, "The Globalization of Artificial Intelligence: Consequences for the Politics of Environmentalism," *Globalizations* 18 (2) (2021): 285–99.

9. Greer is quoted in Alfred Ng, "Facial Recognition's Fate Could Be Decided in 2021," *CNET*, December 11, 2020 (https://www.cnet.com).

10. Naomi Oreskes and Erik M. Conway, *Merchants of Doubt: How a Handful of Scientists Obscured the Truth on Issues from Tobacco Smoke to Global Warming* (Bloomsbury, 2011); Peter Dauvergne, *Will Big Business Destroy Our Planet?* (Polity, 2018); Joel Bakan, *The New Corporation: How "Good" Corporations Are Bad for Democracy* (Vintage Books, 2020); Peter Dauvergne, *AI in the Wild: Sustainability in the Age of Artificial Intelligence* (MIT Press, 2020).

11. Susan George, *Shadow Sovereigns: How Global Corporations Are Seizing Power* (Polity, 2017); John Mikler, *The Political Power of Global Corporations* (Polity, 2018).

12. Peter Dauvergne and Jane Lister, *Eco-Business: A Big-Brand Takeover of Sustainability* (MIT Press, 2013).

13. Peter Dauvergne and Genevieve LeBaron, *Protest Inc.: The Corporatization of Activism* (Polity, 2014).

14. Leon V. Sigal, *Negotiating Minefields: The Landmines Ban in American Politics* (Routledge, 2006); Richard M. Price, *The Chemical Weapons Taboo* (Cornell University Press, 1997); Bill Berry, *Banning DDT: How Citizen Activists in Wisconsin Led the Way* (State Historical Society of Wisconsin, 2014).

Index

"About Face" campaign 51
Access Now 7, 8, 56, 90, 91
    calls for permanent ban of FRT
        11
    role in "Ban Facial Recognition"
        campaign 26
ACLU *see* American Civil Liberties
    Union
ADC *see Asociación por los
    Derechos Civiles*
Africa
    anti-FRT movement 91–2
    facial recognition markets in 84
    resistance to FRT from 9, 31,
        52, 92
AI *see* artificial intelligence
Albania Declaration (2019) 30–31,
    51, 52, 56
Algorithmic Justice League 6–8, 90
Alipay 74
Amazon 35, 37, 50
    calls to commit to never selling
        face surveillance products
        52
    lobbying against municipal laws
        20
    lobbying for industry-oriented
        regulation 14, 59
    pressing for industry-friendly
        national regulation 48
    Rekognition software 48–9, 65,
        89
    stopping sales of facial
        recognition tool 13, 52
Amazon Web Services (AWS) 48
American biometrics software firms
    59, 66
American Civil Liberties Union
    (ACLU) 6, 7, 8, 34, 52, 90

American technology firms 42
Amnesty International 7–8, 16, 22,
    25, 26
    awareness of dangers of face
        surveillance technology 57
    banning use of live facial
        recognition in US 53
    calls for permanent bans of FRT
        9, 11, 90–91
anti-FRT movement 10–11, 16,
    21, 85–6, 92 *see also* facial
    recognition technology (FRT)
    calls for guidelines and guardrails
        27–8
    cooperation and strong
        messaging 28–30
    extending power and reach of
        anti-FRT activism 90–92
    global resistance 23–6, 30–31
    growing influence of anti-FRT
        norm 11–13
    influence of 13–15
    political power of 86
    power of diversity 22–3
    transnational social movements
        21–2
Article 19 7, 8, 9, 90
artificial intelligence (AI) 2, 45, 68
    AI Now Institute 40, 41
    AI-powered facial recognition
        software 70, 72, 73
    Artificial Intelligence Principles 41
Asia-Pacific
    anti-FRT movement 91–2
    facial recognition markets in
        84, 85
    FRT across 77–9
    resistance to FRT from 9, 31,
        52, 92

Asociación por los Derechos Civiles (ADC) 56
Australia, facial recognition technology in 79
authoritarian regimes/states 16, 21, 50
automated facial identification/ recognition 2, 3, 5, 17, 20
AWS *see* Amazon Web Services
Axon 41, 112
Ayonix 66

Baker, Charlie 37, 39, 111
"Ban Automated Recognition of Gender and Sexual Orientation" campaign 9
"Ban Biometric Surveillance" campaign 8–9, 55
"Ban Facial Recognition" campaign 26, 92
"Ban the Scan" campaign 8
Bedoya, Alvaro 6, 101
Bezos, Jeff 49 *see also* Amazon
Biden, Joe 4, 50
Big Brother Watch 7, 8, 9, 53, 83, 90
biometric database 3, 4–5, 78
Biometric Information Privacy Act 13, 63, 119
Black Lives Matter movement 7, 49, 92
Bolsonaro, Jair 56
Boston Globe 39
Brazil
    face surveillance resistance in 56
    facial recognition technology in 85
Brazilian Institute for Consumer Protection *see* Instituto Brasileiro de Defesa do Consumidor (IDEC)
Brazil, Russia, India, China, and South Africa (BRICS) 57
BRICS *see* Brazil, Russia, India, China, and South Africa
Buolamwini, Joy 6, 100

Cagle, Matt 34, 109
Cahn, Albert Fox 48, 114

Carson, Jann 20, 105
cashless economy 74
Castro, Daniel 27, 35, 100, 109
CBP *see* US Customs and Border Protection
CCTV surveillance system *see* closed-circuit television surveillance system
Chau, Ed 47
Cheatham, Renee 32
China
    face-scan economy 74–5
    facial recognition firms 73
    facial recognition market and 3–4
    facial recognition politics in 69–70
    using FRT 2, 13
    FRT in schools 72–4
    role in exporting face surveillance 67–8
    surveillance and policing 70–72
    technology firms in 59
Chow, Kon Yeow 78, 125
Chrispin, Eddy 40, 111
civil liberties 4, 7, 8, 15, 23, 25, 26, 28, 31, 33, 39
civil rights 28, 31, 39, 49, 62, 90, 92–4
civil society
    activism 16
    campaigns across Europe 89
    opposition to face surveillance 53
    organizations 26, 31, 51, 53, 90
    resistance to FRT 35, 55, 79
Clearview AI 89, 120
    controversy 62–4
    story of 59–62
closed-circuit television surveillance system (CCTV surveillance system) 67, 70, 78, 84
CloudWalk 2, 67, 99
CNIL *see Commission Nationale de l'Informatique et des Libertés*
Cognitec 66
Commission Nationale de l'Informatique et des Libertés (CNIL) 54

Communist Party of China 70, 73
Conservation International 92
contentious politics 16
corporate politics of facial recognition
    see also politics of facial
    recognition technology
    Clearview AI role in 59–62
    Clearview controversy 62–4
    exporting face surveillance 67–8
    in facial recognition industry 65
corporate social responsibility (CSR)
    90, 91, 96
Covid-19 pandemic 3, 32, 51, 64, 71,
    73, 77, 79, 87, 90
Coyle, Stefanie 32–3, 108
CSR *see* corporate social
    responsibility
Cuomo, Andrew 33
Cusick, John 83, 127
"Czech Republic, Reclaim Your
    Face" campaign in 9, 52

data privacy laws 54
Day, Tim 48, 114
Delcker, Janosch 55
developing world
    resisting face surveillance in
        55–7
digital images 5
digital rights 26, 31, 34, 51, 57, 90, 91
diversity, power of 22–3

Earthjustice 92
economic(s)
    of facial recognition 86–7
    globalization 17
Ecuador, Chinese-made facial
    recognition technology in 67,
    85
EDPD *see* European Data Protection
    Board
EDRi *see* European Digital Rights
EHRC *see* Equality and Human
    Rights Commission
Electronic Frontier Foundation 6, 7, 8,
    51, 90, 99

Electronic Privacy Information Center
    7, 25, 26, 30, 90
emotion recognition technology 3, 4
Engardio, Joel 36, 109
Enonchong, Rebecca 86, 128
environmentalism 92
Environmental Law Defender Center
    92
Equality and Human Rights
    Commission (EHRC) 53
Etzioni, Oren 83, 127
EU *see* European Union
Europe
    anti-FRT movement in 86
    FRT in 83–4
    resistance to face surveillance in
        53–5
European Data Protection Board
    (EDPD) 12, 63, 89
European Data Protection Supervisor
    12, 89
European Digital Rights (EDRi) 26
    calls for permanent ban on FRT
        11
    network 7, 52
European Union (EU) 8
European Union Agency for
    Fundamental Rights 54

Facebook 13, 38, 60, 62
FacePRO 83
face-scan economy 74–5
face surveillance 25
    Chinese role in export 67–8
    global resistance to 51–2
    resistance in developing world
        55–7
    resistance in Europe 53–5
facial analysis 99–100
    cameras 56
    of police interrogations 91
    software/technology 2, 5, 27,
        73, 76
facial authentication 3, 4, 5, 27, 50, 65
facial identification 4–5
facial payment 74
facial recognition cameras 76

authorities installing 70
detectives using 70
in low-income rental housing
projects 71
mandatory in public areas 56
schools installing 3
security forces mounting 3
facial recognition regulation
denouncing Washington State's
facial recognition
regulation 46–7
model bill 44–5
politics of Microsoft 45–6
politics of regulation in United
States 47–50
Senator Nguyen's facial
recognition law 43–4
facial recognition technology (FRT)
2, 5, 24, 38, 44, 53 *see also*
anti-FRT movement
act of European Commission to
control 12
applications (apps) 60, 77
in Asia-Pacific 77–9
bill 37–8
in China 2–3
criticism of 4–6
Delta Air Lines integrated 80
deployment plan for 93
drones 3
global demand for 76–7
globalization of 83–6
governments restriction to use
89–90
growing facial recognition
market 3–4
in IBM 14
legal and ethical consequences
15–18
Nguyen's facial recognition law
43–4
normalization of 15
in North America 79–83
politics of 15, 86–7
power of activism to resist 94–6
resistance against 7–11, 23–6,
50, 53

sale stoppage in Amazon 13
in schools 72–4
toilet paper dispensers 69
tool in Facebook 13
transnational social movement to
control 10
uneven influence 92–4
United States activities to ban 20,
36–42
uses of 5, 15, 20, 77
facial verification and authentication 4
FBI *see* Federal Bureau of
Investigation
FDC *see* Forum for Democratic
Change
Federal Bureau of Investigation (FBI)
42
Ferguson, Andrew Guthrie 76, 125
Ferrara, Nick 61, 119
"Fight for the Future" organization 7,
8, 20, 40, 62, 91
"Ban Facial Recognition"
campaign 26, 52, 92, 93–4
about FRT 25
FindFace Security 66
Finnie, John 53, 117
Floyd, George 38, 49, 51
Forum for Democratic Change (FDC)
85
France
banning of FRT 53
CNIL supporting data privacy
laws 54
"Reclaim Your Face" campaign
9, 52
Thales Group 59, 65
Freedom House 52, 53, 56
"Friends of the Earth" movement 92
FRT *see* facial recognition technology
"function creep" concept 18

Gates, Kelly 15
General Data Protection Regulation
13, 54, 64
Germany
Cognitec 66

"Face Recognition Stop"
    coalition 53
"Reclaim Your Face" campaign
    9, 52
Gershgorn, Dave 46, 80
Giuliani, Rudy 60
Glaser, Rob 82–3, 126, 127
globalization of facial recognition
    technology 16, 18, 83–6
    charging forward in Asia-Pacific
        77–9
    politics and economics of facial
        recognition 86–7
    rising uptake in North America
        79–83
Global Witness 92
Gomez, Jimmy 49, 115
González, Carlos 39, 111
Good, John 61
Google 38, 41, 60, 62, 96
Greenpeace International 92
Greenpeace USA 16, 22, 92
Guliani, Neema Singh 40
Guo, Bing 74
Gupta, Apar 57, 118

Hartzog, Woodrow 6, 24
Hayes, Myaisha 25, 106
Hill, Kashmir 61, 62
Holland, Lia 20, 105, 119
Hooper, Ibrahim 25, 106
human rights 4, 7–9, 23, 25, 26, 28,
    31, 90, 91
Human Rights Watch 7, 8, 11, 16, 22,
    26, 57, 85, 90, 91

IBM 14, 28, 41, 49, 65, 89
ICE *see* US Immigration and Customs
    Enforcement
IDEC *see* *Instituto Brasileiro de
    Defesa do Consumidor*
IFF *see* Internet Freedom Foundation
India
    Citizenship Act 78–9
    FRT systems in 57, 78
    Internet Freedom Foundation 7,
        8, 9, 31, 55, 57, 90

Information Technology and
    Innovation Foundation 27, 47
Institute of Race Relations 53
*Instituto Brasileiro de Defesa do
    Consumidor* (IDEC) 8, 11, 26
Internal Revenue Service 50
International Civil Liberties
    Monitoring Group 25
Internet Freedom Foundation (IFF)
    7–9, 11, 26, 31, 55, 57, 90
Internet Protocol (IP) 82
Interpol 61
iOmniscient 66
IP *see* Internet Protocol
Italian Data Protection Authority 54
Italy
    Italian Data Protection Authority
        54
    "Reclaim Your Face" campaign
        9, 52

Japan, facial recognition technology
    in 77
jaywalking 2
Jones, Jennifer 24

Kanga, Rustom 66, 121
Kasana, Mehreen 46
Korn, Jonathan W. 76, 125
Krishnan, Anitha 78

Lao, Dongyan 75
Latin America
    anti-FRT movement 91–2
    facial recognition markets in
        84, 85
    resistance to FRT from 9, 31,
        52, 92
law enforcement agencies, use of FRT
    in 9, 12, 24, 38, 40, 42, 52, 93
Leahy, Mark 38, 110
Li, Xiaoyu 2
Liberty 7, 9, 13, 25, 53, 90
Lima, Cristiano 55
live facial recognition cameras 4, 13
    Metropolitan Police of Greater
        London deploying 83

pressure for total ban of 27
testing for US law enforcement
42
UK government to ban use of 53
violating principle of policing by
consent 53–4

Madrid Privacy Declaration (2009) 8
Malaysia, facial recognition
technology in 78
markets for facial recognition 84, 93,
95
Markey, Edward J. 40, 42
Massachusetts 36–40
Matranga, Mike 81, 125
Maynard H. Jackson International
Terminal 80
Megvii 59, 67
Merkley, Jeff 40, 111, 111
Microsoft Corporation 35, 44, 50
decision to stop selling FRT 49,
52
industry-friendly regulations for
FRT 28
lobbying for industry-oriented
regulation 14, 59
politics of 45–6
proposed facial recognition
legislation in California 47
restrained development of FRT
89
model bill 44–5, 51
Modi, Narendra 78
Museveni, Yoweri 84–5

NAACP 47
NEC Corporation 35, 45, 59, 65, 115
NetChoice 37–8, 48
NGOs *see* nongovernmental
organizations
N'Guessan, Charlette 85
Nguyen, Joe 43–4
nongovernmental organizations
(NGOs) 16
nonprofit organizations 22, 47, 52
North America, FRT in 79–80
in airports 80

in basketball's Dallas Mavericks
80–81
in Delta Air Lines 80
in Madison Square Garden 80
in Maynard H. Jackson
International Terminal 80
in residential and commercial
buildings 81
SAFR system 82–3
in Texas City Independent
School District 81–2
in US Customs and Border
Protection 80
NtechLab 59, 66–7, 84

Occupy Movement (2011) 22
one-to-many matching 5
one-to-one matching 4
online payment services 74
OpenMedia 7, 9, 26
Open Rights Group 53
Our Biometric Future (Gates) 15

Panasonic Corporation 65
policing 4, 5, 89, 91, 93
politics of facial recognition
technology 86–7 *see also*
corporate politics of facial
recognition
bans in United States 36–41
in Microsoft 45–6
regulation in United States 47–50
power of diversity 22–3
privacy 4, 5, 7, 8, 31
Privacy International 53
privacy rights 23 28
private faceprint databases 12
pro-democracy movements 21
Public Voice coalition 7, 8, 30, 90
Punke, Michael 48

racism 29, 40, 43
Rainforest Action Network 92
Rainforest Alliance 92
RCMP *see* Royal Canadian Mounted
Police

"Reclaim Your Face" campaign 8, 9, 52
recognition algorithms 77
regulation of FRT 35, 39, 44–7
Rekognition software 48–9, 65, 89
Rodriguez, Katitza 51
Rosbach, Felix 84, 127
Rosenberg, Tracy 10
Royal Canadian Mounted Police (RCMP) 25, 61, 63
Russia, facial recognition technology in 84–5

"SAFR" system 82–3
San Francisco
    ban on facial recognition technology 36
    history of covert surveillance of civil rights movement 33
    pushback in 35–6
    regulatory standards for new technology 34
Saslow, Kate 55
Schilling, Falko 37, 110
Schwartz, Adam 6
Schwartz, Richard 60
Selinger, Evan 6, 24
semi-automated facial recognition 5
SenseTime 59, 67
Shultz, Jim 32, 108
Singapore, facial recognition technology in 78
Smith, Brad 28, 44–6
Sobyanin, Sergei 67, 121
social media firms 62
social movements
    consequences of 9
    transnational *see* transnational social movements
Spivack, Jameson 50, 115
Stamps, De'Keither 36, 109
Stanley, Jay 6, 100
Stark, Luke 24
startups
    from Africa and Latin America 85
    AI and machine learning 59

Chinese 67
    facial recognition 14, 16, 66
S.T.O.P *see* Surveillance Technology Oversight Project
Stop Crime SF 36
Supervisory Body for Police Information 54
surveillance 5–6, 94, 95
    invasive 4
    mass 8, 91, 93
"surveillance creep" 18, 95
Surveillance Technology Oversight Project (S.T.O.P) 48, 50
Swedish Data Protection Authority 54

Tarr, Bruce 38, 110
"technological mission creep" 18
Technology, Education, Development, Research and Communication (TEDIC) 56
TEDIC *see* Technology, Education, Development, Research and Communication
Thales Group 59, 65
Thiel, Peter 60
Ton-That, Hoan 59–64, 119, 119
Toshiba 65
tracking 5
transnational advocacy networks 21–2, 23
transnational corporations 95–6
transnational social movements 10, 16–18, 21–2, 31, 52, 94
Turinawe, Ingrid 85, 127
Turley, Jonathan 35, 104
Twitter 38, 60, 62–3, 65

UCLA *see* University of California Los Angeles
UN High Commissioner for Human Rights 12, 89
United Kingdom (UK) 83, 87
    and Albania Declaration 30
    beginning to integrate facial recognition 83
    Liberty organization in 7, 25

resistance to face surveillance 52, 53
United States (US)
    "Ban Facial Recognition"
        campaign in 26
    facial recognition creep in 42
    facial recognition software in 6
    Maynard H. Jackson
        International Terminal
        in 80
    opposition to Lockport's facial
        security system in 32–3
    ordinance to Stop Secret
        Surveillance 33–4
    politics of facial recognition
        technology bans in 36–41
    politics of regulation in 47–50
    pushback in San Francisco 35–6
University of California Los Angeles
    (UCLA) 13
US Congress 40, 42
US Customs and Border Protection
    (CBP) 42, 80

US Immigration and Customs
    Enforcement (ICE) 42, 60,
    63, 92

Wang, Jun 2
Wang, Maya 57
Washington State's facial recognition
    regulation 46–7
WeChat Pay 74
western democracies 16, 18
Wheeler, Ted 20, 105, 105
Wolfcom 42
Wong, Steven 78
World Wildlife Fund/World Wide
    Fund for Nature (WWF) 92
WWF *see* World Wildlife Fund/
    World Wide Fund for Nature
Wyden, Ron 62

Xu, Jianzhen 73

Yandex 84

Zhang, Guanchao 3
Zhang, Shaomin 69

Printed and bound by CPI Group (UK) Ltd, Croydon, CR0 4YY

27/10/2024

14580411-0001